# THE POWER
## OF
## SMALL CHOICES

# THE POWER OF SMALL CHOICES

Hilary Brand

Pauline

BOOKS & MEDIA

Boston

**Library of Congress Cataloging-in-Publication Data**

Brand, Hilary.
    Power of small choices / Hilary Brand.
       p. cm.
    Originally published: London : Darton, Longman and Todd, Ltd., 2004.
    Includes bibliographical references.
    ISBN 0-8198-5956-7 (pbk.)
    1. Lent—Study and teaching.  2. Christian life—Study and teaching. 3. Choice (Psychology)—Religious aspects—Christianity—Study and teaching. 4. Shawshank redemption (Motion picture)  5. Babettes gæstebud. I. Title.
  BV85.B65 2006
  242'.34—dc22

                     2005018669

The Scripture quotations contained herein are from the *New Revised Standard Version Bible: Catholic Edition,* copyright © 1989, 1993, Division of Christian Education of the National Council of the Churches of Christ in the United States of America. Used by permission. All rights reserved.

Cover design by Rosana Usselmann

Movie photos courtesy of Photofest www.photofestnyc.com

"P" and PAULINE are registered trademarks of the Daughters of St. Paul.

Originally published in Great Britain by Darton, Longman and Todd, London, U.K., 2004

First U.S. Edition, 2005

Published by Pauline Books & Media, 50 Saint Paul's Avenue, Boston, MA 02130-3491. www.pauline.org

Printed in U.S.A.

Pauline Books & Media is the publishing house of the Daughters of St. Paul, an international congregation of women religious serving the Church with the communications media.

1 2 3 4 5 6 7 8 9                  11 10 09 08 07 06 05

*To my friendly local guinea pigs—Graham, Graham, Jenny, Juliet, Karen, Louise, Megan, Paul, Pete, Pete, Pip, Roger, Rose, Sally, Sarah, Sue, Sue, Sue, Susan, Wendy—who demanded "one of those without whom this book could not be written thingys." You richly deserve it. Above all to Pete, the most devoted and long-suffering guinea pig of them all.*

# CONTENTS

## INTRODUCTION

## WEEK ONE

## WEEK TWO

## WEEK THREE

# WEEK FOUR

# WEEK FIVE

# CONCLUSION

# ADDED EXTRAS

## LEADER'S NOTES

# INTRODUCTION

*Small things really are small,*
*but to be faithful in small things is a big thing.*

— Attributed to St. Augustine

*If you think you're too small to make a difference,*
*you've obviously never been in a room with a mosquito.*

— Michelle Walker

## WHY A LENT COURSE?

Lent is a funny thing. Large segments of Christianity know nothing about it, while others take it for granted. Quite *what* they take for granted, though, varies enormously. For some it is simply a time to give up wine or chocolate, a sort of annual show of willpower. For others it means groups—time to gather with others, hopefully of like mind, and talk about faith for a change, rather than just listening. And like most talking, it isn't particularly intended to *change* anything. Change? Heaven forbid!

So what is Lent meant to be about? Is it just something to fill a gap in that dull section of the Church year, after the nativity figures have been put back in the loft and before the summer vacation season kicks in?

I originally hail from a segment of the Church where Lent doesn't happen, so when I first decided to write a Lent course, I thought I'd better find out where the idea actually came from.

For a start, what does the word mean? Well, nothing to do with borrowing. It is, apparently, based on the old Saxon word *"Lenctentid,"* used for the month of March, and denoting the lengthening of days. Not much help there then.

I eventually discovered that the idea grew up long before the Saxons christened it, in the very first centuries of the Church, when baptisms (and renewal of baptismal vows) were only held at Easter. It was a time of preparation (often including fasting), a time of getting ready to move on—to a new phase, a further stage in the journey.

The forty days came from Jesus, of course, although he did it the other way round—the baptism came first and then the forty days in the wilderness. But the principle was the same. He knew he needed a time of reflection and aloneness in order to be ready for what was to come—though I doubt that he had bargained on quite how challenging a time it would be.

## Time for Challenge

It may be that you haven't bargained on quite how challenging this particular Lent course is.

Firstly, it is mentally challenging. I have tried to make it as user-friendly as possible, but I wanted to explore some very big ideas about choice and about change. I also wanted to take in thoughts from both contemporary culture and scientific thought, so forgive me if at times it becomes a little brain-stretching.

Secondly, it is—or at least I hope so—practically challenging, because, beside the big cosmic thoughts, I wanted to look at life on the tiniest level—what we watch and whom we write to, how we greet strangers, what bananas we pick from the supermarket shelf....

And somewhere in between all that, I wanted to explore what motivates the choices we make (or fail to make) and what suppositions we may need to question and possibly throw out.

Last but not least, I wanted to explore how principles laid down by Jesus (and by the prophets before him and the apostles who followed) had something to say about what it means to be a free human being living responsibly before God.

So I hope this course will be a voyage of exploration for you too—interesting, unusual, and fun. I hope it will awaken for you a fuller understanding of how God made a world with endless creative possibilities, how walking in the way of that God is a unique and purposeful journey for each one of us, and how small choices actually aren't that small at all!

## Time for Variety

People have different ways of exploring their faith. Some prefer theological delving—abstract concepts, big ideas. Some like stories—fictional or real life. Others want poetry, prayer, and stillness. Still others prefer their religion practical—*do this, don't do that*. The Bible understands this brilliantly and offers all these approaches. In a giant foolhardy leap, I decided to try to do the same.

So, although this course is designed so that all its component parts relate to each other to form a coherent whole, some parts may scratch where you itch and others may not. And that's fine.

The course is designed in two main ways—material to be read individually and material for group sessions. Of course, it will be a much richer experience if you can manage to do both. However, it is possible to do one without the other—they are intended to complement rather than directly follow each other.

So feel free to pick and choose what is appropriate to you. Indeed, unless you have the luxury of a wilderness retreat, I may have crammed in far too much material for forty days anyway. But since this course is about choice, I thought it no bad thing that its structure should have an element of choice too!

# HOW TO USE THIS BOOK

## TIME FOR INDIVIDUAL READING

### The Big Picture (Before Group Session)

These five sections explore big ideas about choice— freedom and responsibility, nature and nurture, whether our faith enables or inhibits choice—and a look at how contemporary thought on these issues (often radically different than a Christian worldview) relates to a biblical perspective. Ideally, these are intended to be read weekly as a forerunner to the group sessions.

### The Human Scale (After Group Session)

Big ideas are fascinating, but they are useless unless we act on them. This second strand of five sections focuses on real-life examples of people who have made a difference—sometimes in small spur-of-the-moment actions, sometimes in a life of dogged, long-haul perseverance. They look at how even the biggest ventures spring from small beginnings and at how we might be creative in our choices even within very limited circumstances. These sections might be best read weekly as a follow-up to the group sessions.

## TIME TOGETHER: THE GROUP SESSIONS

There are five weekly sessions, designed to run from the week following Ash Wednesday to the week before Holy Week. You need to have seen the two movies being used in this course beforehand.

Also included are two additional studies on key Bible passages, to be used either for individual reading or possibly for extra group sessions after Easter.

There is also a suggestion for a final event to consolidate and celebrate after the course ends.

### The Group Session Components

The five group outlines use two classic movies as discussion starting points. Each group session uses one clip from each film, going on to link them with Gospel passages and ending with a short time of stillness, prayer, and meditation.

Occasionally, the group outlines link directly to the individual reading matter, but on the whole they are free-standing—and are sufficiently crammed that there is not a great deal of space for bringing in ideas suggested by the other chapters. If you would like to discuss any issues brought up by individual reading, you may need to make space to do so.

## The Films

*The Shawshank Redemption* and *Babette's Feast* are powerful stories in their own right. Although quite different in style and subject matter, both portray the possibility of choice in even the most limited circumstances.

*The Shawshank Redemption,* set in the bleak situation of life imprisonment, is a story of hope and determination overcoming fear. Nominated for seven Academy Awards, it is nevertheless, according to film critic Mark Kermode, "a classic example of a film that succeeded not because people were told by the studios that it was a great movie, but because people told each other it was a great movie."[1] It includes some scenes of violence and the sort of strong language you would expect prisoners to use. (It is rated as suitable for age fifteen and over.) I know that some people prefer not to watch this sort of material. If you are one of them, I hope you will take courage and bear with it. Neither the violence nor the language is gratuitous, but necessary to a realistic portrayal, and I think you will discover that what comes from the story is overwhelmingly positive.

*Babette's Feast,* by contrast, is a very gentle and somewhat slow film set in a remote island community in Denmark. (You may find it available with subtitles or dubbing. Choose subtitles as the better option if possible.) It tells the story of two aging sisters, daughters of a village pastor, who have refused marriage in order to carry on their father's work among his dwindling flock. Into their midst comes Babette, a penniless refugee from the French Revolution, and the story tells what happens when she comes into a little money and decides to throw a feast.

It is possible to participate in group sessions without having seen the films, but it is not recommended. If at all possible, try to see both films before the course starts.

## The Role of Fiction

Some people are uncomfortable with the idea of using fictional stories as a Christian learning tool. "But they're not *true*," they say.

What they mean is that they are not factual. But just because something is fictional rather than an account of real verifiable events doesn't mean it has no truths to teach us. In fact the reverse is often true.

Imagine you were asked to write a history of your family. You wouldn't find it difficult to write the facts: names, addresses, and dates, births, deaths, and marriages. You could assemble photos that run the gamut of important events and trivial moments. But quite probably, and quite rightly, you would choose not to reveal all the harsh reality that underlies those impassive facts and smiling faces. Disappointing marriages, cruel words, sibling rivalries, infidelities, money worries— these things happen in all families, sometimes blatantly, sometimes subtly, often hidden under a veneer of polite respectability. Would you actually put in print how difficult you sometimes find your spouse, your kids, your parents, or your in-laws? It may be that you barely acknowledge these things to yourself. Would you even reveal your golden moments—sex in the firelight, a rare hug from a monosyllabic teenager, the blessed time after Christmas when the visitors leave!

But if you were writing fiction you could do it. You could explore those moments of temptation, the gut-wrench of disillusionment, the little power games that people play, the words that are never ever said. You could try to portray how those times of utter ordinariness—pushing a child on a swing, sweeping the leaves, watching a video with Chinese takeout—are, for most of us, our moments of greatest happiness. It would probably be a far truer account of what it means to be a family than any bald recitation of factual information could ever be.

Now I know you could argue that these films I have chosen are not realistic. Both have simplifications, implausibilities, over-neat endings. You could say that they are fables. But fables—from Aesop to Narnia—have always been told and retold not just because they are enjoyable, but also because they have something powerful to say about being human.

A screenwriter acquaintance of mine describes his calling thus: "I want to make people feel so much that they start to think."

I hope that this course does the same job.

## The Art of Listening

One of the most valuable aspects of groups is learning to listen to each other, understanding where someone else is coming from, and why your particular approach may not be the only one or even a right one at all! This course is about choice and I hope the group sessions will help you to respect and support one another's choices.

---

### The Ground Rules

- Give space for every member of the group who wishes to speak to do so.

- Speak as much as possible from your experience, rather than on a theoretical level.

- Actively listen to each contribution, rather than thinking about what you'd like to say.

- Respect each other's viewpoints and, if possible, try to understand what formed them.

- Make it a rule to keep what is said within the group; make it a safe place to be honest.

Be quick to listen, slow to speak.... But be doers of the word, and not merely hearers who deceive themselves. (James 1:19, 22)

---

# WHY SMALL CHOICES?

Perhaps I'm getting old. Perhaps it's empty-nest syndrome. Perhaps I've just spent too much time recently filling in job applications.

Whatever it is, I often seem to find myself reflecting on the nature of my life.

And what I've been feeling is that it seems quite small.

## A Hill of Beans?

I've found myself feeling rather like the Humphrey Bogart character in *Casablanca,* when he tells Ingrid Bergman that their lives "don't amount to a hill of beans in this crazy world."[2]

Where are the wise statements, the grand gestures, the heroic sacrifices I once thought I might make? What happened to the noble destiny, the shining example I hoped I might be? I have a friend who memorably describes his life as "like the opening break of an amateur billiards player." I know what he means. In the harsh black and white of my curriculum vitae, my life looks like a random scattering of experiment and expediency.

These wallowings in mid-life angst have been disturbed, however, by a bombardment of contrary ideas.

Perhaps it began with my last Lent course, *Chocolate for Lent,* which led me to explore the ethics of buying a chocolate bar.

Perhaps it was provoked by reading Philip Pullman and Richard Dawkins, brilliant storyteller and science writer respectively, who both seem to regard the Church as a destroyer of freedom.

Perhaps it was that troubling parable from Jesus about the man who buried his talent.

Whatever it was, it sent me on a journey of exploration into the whole idea of small choices.

For alongside the feeling that all my life choices have turned out rather insignificant (and my realization that almost everyone else feels the same), has been a growing conviction that actually small choices matter a great deal, that every one of those millions of tiny decisions we make in a lifetime has the potential to change the world.

Does that seem like a ridiculous claim?

Please note: I'm not saying all of them do. Rather that they *could,* and that the consequences of our actions are often much more far-reaching than we're aware of and possibly much greater than we have the power to imagine.

## A Bundle of Neurons

Did you realize that the human brain is the most complex piece of matter in the whole universe? Has it ever occurred to you that you are walking around with the pinnacle of creation in a gelatinous grey lump behind your eyeballs?

The rest of you is pretty amazing too. Did you know that within the nucleus of *each* cell of your body (and you have around 10 trillion of them) is more coded information than all thirty volumes of the *Encyclopedia Britannica* put together?[3]

Did you realize that the likelihood of a universe like ours, capable of sustaining intelligent life, is infinitesimally small? If the force of gravity were even a tiny bit stronger or weaker, if the sun generated just a little more or less energy, if the distances of space were even in the smallest way different, then we wouldn't exist at all. Mathematician Roger Penrose has calculated the probability of a universe ending up exactly like ours as one in ten to the power of 123.[4] That doesn't mean much to me, but I'm told that even if every proton in the entire universe was used to write a digit on (and protons are so small that the dot on this "i" could hold around 500,000,000,000 of them), it couldn't express the number of variant universes possible. Out of all those variations, the universe as it actually turned out is the only possible variant able to sustain life as we know it. And within that universe, so far as we are aware, our insignificant little planet is the only one that actually has life with intelligence. So the fact that we are here at all is pretty amazing.

Now, as some scientists will tell us, all this *could* have happened by blind chance. Or our universe *could* actually be just one of an infinite number. But a far more reasonable explanation seems to me (and to much greater minds than mine) to be that Someone very much wanted us to be here.

Well, that certainly goes some way to making me feel less insignificant.

## A Process of Change

You will see from the above that I've been reading up on my science recently. Now I'm no rocket scientist.

Please don't ask me to explain $e = mc^2$ or Heisenberg's Uncertainty Principle. But even from my limited perspective, I began to wonder whether contemporary understanding of the material world might have something quite important to say about the spiritual life—in particular, about this whole idea of small choices. I hope you'll bear with me as I try and explain what I mean.

Take evolution, for instance. Apart from the obvious—that Darwin's small choice to take a boat to the Galapagos Islands had far-reaching effects he could never have dreamed of—his conclusions have even bigger implications both about small choices and about how God fits in.

(I don't want to get into an Evolution versus Creationism debate here. I have chosen to take the word of almost all bona fide scientists, whether believers or atheists, who accept the evolutionary hypothesis—and, of course, the discovery of DNA makes it far more than a hypothesis. Biology aside, every aspect of science now builds from and confirms the idea of an earth much older than the writers of Genesis could conceive. And although there are some very loud voices proclaiming that science disproves religion, there are also some quiet and more reasoned ones explaining why no conflict exists. And those quiet voices sound pretty convincing to me.)

Anyway, if we accept Darwin's theory, then we begin to understand that creatures like us exist, not through an instantaneous wave of a divine magic wand, but through a process involving millions of cumulative tiny changes.

And if the earth did not spring into existence ready-made, but is still being created in a continuing process, then any idea that God set the whole thing going and left us to get on with it goes out of the window. Creation is an ongoing activity. God is involved in every moment of change, in every latent possibility.

So if we accept that God designed the natural world this way, it is reasonable to suppose that he designed our lives this way also. What seem like tiny insignificant actions to us may well be part of a much greater plan and purpose. Experiment and expediency don't seem quite so unspiritual. Mistakes may be turned to good use. Chance becomes opportunity. We may begin to see ourselves as part of what physicist and theologian John Polkinghorne describes as "a universe endowed with becoming."[5] We will start to understand that God made us not just to be, but to become.

## An Ancient Wisdom

Of course, it's all there in Genesis anyway.

Well, no, not evolution. But an understanding of what it means to be human that complements and goes beyond what even today's science with all its wonders can give us.

Some misunderstand the Old Testament these days—certainly outside of church, but in my observation, quite often inside as well. And, if it is read simplistically, no wonder. We don't go too far through its pages before we trip across divine anger, tribal vengeance, weird rules, and sexist men—a Bronze Age world, in fact, with all that entails. But they knew a thing or two, those Bronze-Age scribes and chieftains, that we could sometimes do well to explore.

Take that first chapter, that wonderful rolling litany of delight, with its evocative refrain: "And God saw that it was good. And there was morning and evening, the first/second/third (etc.) day."

There we are on the sixth day, humans—amazing god-like creatures—that God sees are "very good." In fact, not only are we amazing and god-like, but also we're commissioned to "rule over" all the rest.

Not a popular concept, this "ruling over." On it have been blamed many of the world's ecological ills, in an assumption that it gives humankind a license to plunder and squander and destroy the earth's resources with impunity, because it says that we are "in control." We are in charge. We can choose. We can rule wisely or badly, respectful of the rest of creation or disdainful of it. But what that verse tells us more profoundly is that "rule" is not something humans have usurped. It is what we have been given. It is given not just to Adam, or the Queen of England, or the President of the United States of America, but to all of us. It is a responsibility that comes with being the god-like creature that each of us is. We shirk it at our peril.

## A Very Important Word

Of course, Genesis almost immediately complicates this god-like status by bringing in another unpopular word: "sin." No, not in the Garden in chapter 3 where the word is not mentioned. (More of that puzzling story later, particularly in the Added Extras section on page 181.)

In fact, it first appears in chapter 4, where it is described in terms of a crouching animal ready to devour the jealous Cain. "Its desire is for you," says the Lord to Cain, who is furious that his brother, Abel, is more favored, "but you must master it." Or at least, that's how my Bible translation, the *New Revised Standard Version,* puts it.

The author John Steinbeck explores this verse in one of his greatest novels, *East of Eden.*[6] One of the characters, Adam, has twin sons, and when it comes to naming them, there is a discussion with his Chinese servant, Lee, as to why no children are ever named after Cain, son of the first Adam.

Many years later, Lee tells how that discussion sent him back to look at the ancient story and on a long quest of understanding. What provoked it was his discovery that in the *King James Version* of the Bible the phrase is rendered as a promise: "and thou shalt rule over him." (Curiously, it is sin that is referred to in personal terms as "him.") However, in the *American Standard Bible,* newly published at the time of the novel's setting, it is very different. The verse says, "Do thou rule over him." It is not a promise, but an order.

These differences fascinate Lee, who eventually travels to San Francisco to explore them with a group of Chinese sages. After two years of discussion and study, plus bringing in a Jewish rabbi and learning Hebrew, they eventually reach a conclusion:

> "My old gentlemen felt that these words were very important too—'Thou shalt' and 'Do thou.' And this was the gold from our mining: 'Thou mayest.' Thou mayest rule over sin...."

He explains that the original Hebrew word *timshel* is literally translated as "Thou mayest":

> "Don't you see?... 'Thou mayest'—that gives a choice. It might be the most important word in the world. That says the way is open. That throws it right back on a man. For if 'Thou mayest'—it is also true that 'Thou mayest not'..."

Lee's friends still can't grasp why Lee, for whom the Bible is not a divine book, is so excited about the discovery. He explains how the two other interpretations of the phrase can lead either to blind obedience or passive acceptance of fate:

> "But 'Thou mayest'! Why, that makes a man great, that gives him stature with the gods, for in his weakness and in his filth and in his murder of his brother he still has the great choice. He can choose his course and fight it through and win...

"It is easy, out of laziness, out of weakness to throw oneself into the lap of deity, saying, 'I couldn't help it. The way was set.' But think of the glory of the choice! That makes a man a man.... This—this is a ladder to climb to the stars."

Think of the glory of the choice! Of course, that may leave you thinking that you have very little scope for choice, and, if so, then you are probably not alone. But maybe, as this book goes on, you will begin to see that your small choices have far more potential than you could possibly realize. And that even if you've not been exercising your choice much lately, it's never too late to start.

God didn't make us with all that brainpower for nothing!

—

I praise you, for I am fearfully and wonderfully made (Ps 139:14).

## WEEK ONE

*The only thing you know for sure is the present tense...*
*The "nowness" of everything is absolutely wondrous...*
*The fact is that if you see the present tense,*
*boy, do you see it, and boy can you celebrate it!*

— Dennis Potter

*He who would do good to another must do it in*
*minute particulars. General good is the plea of the*
*scoundrel, hypocrite, and flatterer. For Art and Science*
*cannot exist but in minutely organized particulars.*

— William Blake

# THE BIG PICTURE
## FAITH: FREEDOM OR STRAITJACKET?

### God: Friend or Foe?

In a recent British TV drama, *The Second Coming,* an ordinary Manchester bloke-at-the-pub called Steve finds himself suddenly transformed into the Son of God. He proclaims that there is to be a "Third Testament," which people should write themselves. Suggestions flood in, but none of them seems right—until his girlfriend invites him round and offers him poisoned casserole, telling him she has figured this is the answer. Her explanation is simple:

> "My testament says that you die, that you go.... The existence of God has destroyed us, so it stops because I say so.... The end of this world and the start of a new one without religion on our backs."
>
> "And what sort of world would that be?"
>
> "Better...cos right now we're promised an afterlife, so we waste the seventy years we've got. If God is dead though, and this is all we've got, maybe we'll use it.... Soon as we get rid of God, that's when we grow up.... It was in your big speech. It was there all along. You said we've got to take responsibility and if you really want us to do that, then we've got to do it on our own."[1]

The playwright Russell T. Davies clearly believes that having faith hinders responsible choice and his voice is not the only one promoting the idea. Children's author Philip Pullman agrees, and famously in his *His Dark Materials* trilogy, he floats the idea of a "republic of heaven":

> We have to build the republic of heaven where we are, because for us there is no elsewhere... He [Lord Asriel] meant the kingdom of heaven was over, the kingdom of heaven, it was all finished. We shouldn't live as if it mattered more than life in this world, because where we are is always the most important place....[2]

David Boulton, former head of current affairs at Granada TV, took up this idea in an article in *The Guardian,* writing of "a republic where the public is king—where we have to take responsibility for creating a better world 'as it is in heaven,' instead of leaving it all to the Authority."[3] It's interesting that after examining what such a republic might look like, he concluded: "To my surprise I find it not very different from the kingdom of heaven described by Jesus a couple of thousand years ago." Curiously, Pullman too, though asserting that God is dead and the only life we have is here, has little argument with Jesus, saying (in a *South Bank Show* interview) that "If only the Church had listened to the Beatitudes and if only the people had listened to Jesus instead of the priests who came after him, we'd all be a lot better off."[4]

So what is it then that these guys are getting at? Do they have a point? Would human life be more vibrant, more responsible, without God, the Church, or the afterlife?

## Heaven: Help or Hindrance?

I'm not sure what I believe about heaven. Harps and clouds don't appeal to me and sometimes I think I'd be quite happy for my molecules to be subsumed into the general matter of the cosmos. Sometimes I can't imagine ceasing to exist as a conscious being on earth. Sometimes it seems like quite a good idea!

So I don't think the idea of an afterlife too much informs my choices now...except that in the Gospels, Jesus tells me, and I believe him, that wherever I subsequently "float off to" and in whatever form, I will one day—perhaps tomorrow, perhaps forty years hence—have to meet my Maker and give an account of myself. There are times (for instance, in the story of the sheep and the goats in Matthew 25, or the rich man and the beggar in Luke 16) when Jesus describes that Maker as somewhat ruthless to those who have chosen to ignore him (or more importantly perhaps, ignore their neighbor), and I'll admit that bothers me.

But to those who reach out to him, the description is of a gentle and generous Father—inviting requests, welcoming home the wayward, strengthening the weak, and healing the hurt. Over several decades of attempting to follow his way, I have found that description to be true. I have seen requests granted (not always exactly as I asked, but always for the good), I have experienced strength flow in when I thought I had none, I have felt the slate wiped clean...and the relief of homecoming when things have gone wrong.

And in the end, I would say that all of those things have enhanced the importance of my daily choices and my capacity to make them. To me, the experience of God has been liberating rather than limiting.

Nevertheless, I think I can understand some of what those critics of religion have in mind.

## Guidance: Liberation or Limitation?

Guidance is a sticky issue. Does it mean that God only has one path for us, so that if we miss it, that's our whole life gone down the drain? Does it mean we have to hear a clear set of directions, or wait "in limbo" until we do?

I have already said that I believe God has answered my requests. And some of those requests have been for guidance. There have been times when I have felt sure God was making the next step clear. (No words booming from the sky, though sometimes coming unbidden into my head. No prophetic utterances, though sometimes the suggestion of a friend or some lines on a page. No miracles, though plenty of coincidences.)

But there have also been times when no answer has been forthcoming. For a long while that puzzled me. Had my relationship with God dried up?

It was the following statement from a discussion about science and faith that set me thinking: "If God came and made the divine will so absolutely clear that no one could possibly doubt it, it would cause grave problems for the idea that we have freedom."[5] The speaker went on to describe how absurd it would be in an exam situation if the teacher stood right behind the pupil muttering the right answer in his or her ear all the time. He explained that he believes it to be a part of the scheme of things that God sometimes hides himself from us.

> To be a hand's breadth off, to allow us to be free—but creating that gracious atmosphere that encourages us to be creative and to respond, providing that stimulating ambience so that we are urged on....
>
> God's problem, if I may put it like that, is to create a world which can be itself. If there is to be love which responds to God, God has to stand back in order to allow the world to be itself, to allow the love that flows back to him to be free.

I found that idea of God standing back very helpful. It reminded me of when we taught our kids to ride a bike. If you are a parent you will understand. You run along behind them holding on and they're saying, "Don't let go. Don't let go!" And you say, "It's all right. I'm here. I'm holding on." But of course, there comes a point when you know they're ready and you let go of the bike and they go pedaling off—until they realize and wobble a bit and stop. And then they get cross and say, "But you let go. You said you wouldn't." And you say, "Yeah, but look, you did it. You rode the bike!"

So I'm learning that silence does not necessarily mean absence, that God may not be holding the bike but he's still making sure I'm safe. I'm beginning to get a grip on this interactive business. It's not just me requesting and God answering. Sometimes it's God opening up a space for me to participate—for me to actually do the choosing, letting me be grown up enough to decide where to go or what to do.

## Decisions: Dependence or Dignity?

So I do still believe in guidance, but I hold it rather more lightly.

And I wonder if it's at those times when we cling to the idea of guidance more desperately than we ought to that things start to go wrong. Because if we are too dependent on having it all spelled out, there are likely to be at least four dodgy outcomes:

- It may stifle us. We may never take a step in any direction for fear of being wrong.

- It may cause us to resort to spiritual trickery such as: Putting a finger in the Bible and seeing what text comes up (you may have heard the old preacher's tale of the man who tried that and arrived at Matthew 27:5: "he went and hanged himself," tried again and got to Luke 10:37: "Go and do likewise"); or asking for a sign (like the woman who went as a missionary to South America on the strength of being given a box of chocolate brazils).

- It may cause us to depend too much on the wrong authority. If we can't allow God to be silent on an issue, then we may turn too quickly to his human agents to help us out. There are plenty out there—counselors, priests, preachers, self-help books, theological expositions. Their advice may be sound, their moral laws may be wise, and, if so, they are a resource to be used. But there are quite a few charlatans out there, sometimes very charismatic (note the small "c"), and not a few control freaks. I'd suggest that a good rule of thumb might be: *The keener someone is to tell you what to do, the more cautious you should be.* Listen to what others say by all means, but never forget that God gave you the ability to weigh it. Jesus came to set you free, not to tie you up. And that includes freedom in making decisions. (I don't mean that submission and humility are not part of the picture— indeed, they are vital components in Jesus' topsy-turvy kingdom—rather that they, too, are chosen, practiced with the same dignity with which Jesus faced his cross.)

Philip Pullman understands what can go wrong if you let others do the choosing. At the end of the final book in *His Dark Materials* trilogy, an angel named Xaphania tells Will, the young protagonist, that he must return to his own world, because he has an important task to do there.

"What work have I got to do then?" said Will, but went on at once. "No, on second thought, don't tell me. I shall decide what I do. If you say my work is fighting or healing or exploring or whatever you might say, I'll always be thinking about it, and if I do end up doing that I'll be resentful because it'll feel as if I didn't have a choice and if I don't do it, I'll feel guilty because I should. Whatever I do, I will choose it, no one else."

"Then you have already taken the first steps toward wisdom," said Xaphania.[6]

## Destiny: Here and Now

Something else we can learn from Pullman is his insistence that "where we are is always the most important place...." It may not be the afterlife that stymies our choices, but the idea that just around the corner in this life is some great new opportunity that God has waiting for us. Or that at some time in the past, we got it irretrievably wrong. Whatever God might have waiting for us in the future, whatever we might have missed or grasped in the past, right now *this is all we have*. There are opportunities all around us right now, if only we can see them.

Strangely enough, I suspect that great Old Testament visionary Moses might have agreed with Pullman on this one. When, as an old man, he had led the people to the brink of the Promised Land, Moses made one last impassioned plea. In a speech of Martin Luther King or Nelson Mandela eloquence, he pleaded

with the people to hold on to the new beliefs and prac-
tices instilled in them in the wilderness. He feared they
would not, and poignantly knew he would not be there
to see it. He ends the speech with a final thundering
challenge:

> "I call heaven and earth to witness against you today
> that I have set before you life and death, blessings
> and curses. Choose life so that you and your descen-
> dants may live, loving the LORD your God, obeying
> him, and holding fast to him; for that means life to
> you..." (Dt 30:19–20).

The genius of Moses as a leader was that, although he
understood that faith needed grand statements ("Now
choose life"), clear symbols (tablets of stone, the Ark of
the Covenant), and the remembrance of defining
moments (the Passover, the Red Sea crossing), he also
knew that where the life of faith really lay was in the little things.

It lay in your financial transactions, in what you ate
or wore, when you worked and when you relaxed, in
your family relations, your sexual activity, your dealings
with strangers. And although some of the Old
Testament laws may seem abstruse and overly prescrip-
tive to us, it's worth remembering what a giant leap forward in understanding they actually were. Back in
Egypt, religion was all about magic and mystery, idols
and sacrifice. It had no direct link to everyday ethics; in
fact, much of its morality was distinctly dubious! The

amazing leap forward made during those wilderness wanderings was firstly to grasp the idea of one God and, secondly, to understand how that one God was involved in every aspect of life. The nitty-gritty rulebook of 3,000 years ago is understandably odd to us. What is so wonderful is that it *is* nitty-gritty!

I suspect that Moses may have also grasped something else important: that the small choices of life are often just as difficult as the big ones. In fact, the big ones—the Red Sea moments—often seem inevitable, the logical conclusion to all those small ones.

## Law: Oppression or Option

"Now choose life," thundered Moses, knowing that the choosing would lay in what to do when your neighbor's ox strayed, or a stranger wandered across your field, or your neighbor invited you to a jolly feast around a symbolic totem pole, or your sister-in-law was left a widow.

Anyone who took on those laws in their entirety today would be odd indeed. (And oddly enough, such people appear to exist—although in practice even the most vehement of them is highly selective.) The Old Testament Law had a vital purpose in its time and as the basis for all three monotheistic religions deserves immense respect, as Jesus clearly shows.

But Jesus also came with a determined mission to take faith right out of any legalistic straitjacket. Of course, down the ages there seem to have been a remarkable number of people claiming his authority and equally determined to tie faith up again! I'm not one of them. However, I do wonder what our world would look like if people now began to look closely at those laws, worked out the principles behind them, and then opted to apply those principles to the choices of today: what they watched on TV, what they put in their supermarket cart, which politician they voted for. I suspect there might be great improvement.

—

Work out your own salvation with fear and trembling; for it is God who is at work in you, enabling you both to will and to work for his good pleasure (Phil 2:12–13).

# GROUP SESSION
## THE CHOICE OF OBSERVATION

***Introducing Ourselves***                     *5–10 min.*

Why have you chosen to come to this course? What would you like to get out of it?

***Introducing the Ground Rules***                *1 min.*

- Give space for every member of the group who wishes to speak to do so.

- Speak as much as possible from your experience, rather than at a theoretical level.

- Actively listen to each contribution, rather than thinking about what you'd like to say.

- Respect each other's viewpoints and if possible try to understand what formed them.

- Make it a rule to keep what is said within the group; make it a safe place to be honest.

## Introduction to *Babette's Feast*

Two devout aging sisters, Phillipa and Martina, have devoted their lives to continuing their pastor father's work, serving their remote community on the Danish coast. Some years ago they took in Babette, a penniless refugee from the French Revolution, to be their maid. Now Babette, who was once a chef in Paris, comes into some money and offers to cook a feast for the dwindling

group of believers to celebrate the pastor's memory. The austere community accepts the offer, but they are worried. They make up their minds that the sensory pleasures of the feast will not tempt them to their downfall. However, General Löwenhielm, an unexpected visitor from the Danish court, has another perspective.

*Clip 1: Babette's Feast*                          *4 min.*
*At the feast: "Remember we have lost our sense of taste."*

*Discuss*                                         *5–10 min.*
Two vastly different attitudes toward food here: one that it is of no importance and that we shouldn't dwell on it, the other that we should savor it to the full. Is one more Christian than the other and, if so, why? What are the pitfalls of both views if taken to extremes?

Reader 1: Luke 12:16–31                          *3 min.*

Then he told them a parable: "The land of a rich man produced abundantly. And he thought to himself, 'What should I do, for I have no place to store my crops?' Then he said, 'I will do this: I will pull down my barns and build larger ones, and there I will store all my grain and my goods. And I will say to my soul, "Soul, you have ample goods laid up for many years; relax, eat, drink, be merry." ' But God said to him, 'You fool! This very night your life is being demanded of you. And the things you have prepared, whose will they be?' So it is with those who store up treasures for themselves but are not rich toward God."

Reader 2: Matthew 7:7–11

"Ask, and it will be given you; search, and you will find; knock, and the door will be opened for you. For everyone who asks receives, and everyone who searches finds, and for everyone who knocks, the door will be opened. Is there anyone among you who, if your child asks for bread, will give a stone? Or if the child asks for a fish, will give a snake? If you then, who are evil, know how to give good gifts to your children, how much more will your Father in heaven give good things to those who ask him!"

***Discuss***                                  ***3–5 min.***

What light, if any, do these sayings of Jesus cast on the issue?

***Ponder and Share***                    ***5–10 min.***

The passage from Matthew talks about God wanting to give us good things. Our lives are probably crammed with good things, but how much do we appreciate them? How much did you savor the meal you had before this session? What did you notice in the natural world around you today—trees, birds, colors, the sky, scents, tastes?

*Brainstorm*                                          *5–10 min.*

Create two lists:

List one: What affects your choices from the supermarket shelf?

List two: What factors affect the way you choose to eat your food?

What background values affect these choices?

⚊

## Introduction to *Shawshank Redemption*

A change of gear now, from awareness and appreciation of food to awareness of others. We join this film near the beginning where Andy Dufresne has just been committed to life imprisonment for a murder he claims he never committed. As you might expect, the prison world is harsh and violent with strong language, and this clip reflects that.

*Clip 2: Shawshank Redemption*                        *8 min.*
*Betting on which new arrival in prison breaks down first.*

*Discuss*                                          *10–15 min.*

This is a pretty brutal sequence. How many of you would normally choose not to watch something like this?

If not, why not? How can you ensure you are not getting divorced from reality?

If you do choose to watch violent on-screen material, what is your reason? How can you ensure you don't get desensitized? What boundaries, if any, have you decided to set?

The question "What was his name?" is an affront to the other inmates. Why?

**Ponder and Share**                                    *5–7 min.*
Think about what preoccupations prevented you from noticing fully your environment and the people who were around you today.

**Meditation**                                          *5–7 min.*

**Silence**                                    *30 sec.–1 min.*

Reader 3: Two readings from the great spiritual writer Henri Nouwen:

> It is hard to live in the present. The past and the future keep harassing us. The past with guilt, the future with worries.... Guilt that says: "You ought to have done something other than what you did; you ought to have said something other than what you said." These "oughts" keep us feeling guilty about the past and prevent us being fully present to the moment.
>
> Worse, however, than our guilt are our worries. Our worries fill our lives with "What ifs": "What if I lose my job; what if my father dies; what if there is not enough money...?" These

many "ifs" can so fill our mind that we become blind to the flowers in the garden and the smiling children on the streets, or deaf to the grateful voice of a friend.

The real enemies of our life are the "oughts" and the "ifs." They pull us back to the unalterable past and forward into the unpredictable future. But real life takes place in the here and the now. God is a God of the present. God is always in the moment, be that moment hard or easy, joyful or painful.[7]

*Silence*                                    *30 sec.–1 min.*

Reader 4

Imagine that we could live each moment as a moment pregnant with new life. Imagine that we could live each day as a day full of promises. Imagine that we could walk through the new year always listening to a voice saying to us: "I have a gift for you and I can't wait for you to see it." Imagine...

The problem is that we allow our past, which becomes longer and longer each year, to say to us: "You know it all; you have seen it all, be realistic; the future will be just the same as the past. Try to survive it as best you can."

When we listen to these [voices], they eventually prove themselves right: our new year, our new day, our new hour become flat, boring, dull and without anything new.

We must open our minds and hearts to the voice that resounds...saying, "Let me show you where I live among my people. My name is 'God-with-you...'"

We must choose to listen to that voice and every choice will open us a little more to discover the new life hidden in the moment, waiting eagerly to be born.

*Silence*                        *30 sec.–1 min.*

Reader 5: Prayer

    Lord,

    give us a sense of wonder at the world around us.

    Remind us to savor the good things you have
        given,

    to delight in what is there for us right now,

    rather than worrying about what might not be
        there tomorrow.

    Teach us to notice those people you have put in
        our path.

    Help us to find out who they really are and
        what they have to give.

    Lord, teach us to shake off the shadows of the past
    and walk in the light of the now.

    Amen.

*Silence*                        *30 sec.–1 min.*

*Note for Future Discussion*            *1 min.*

Are there any questions arising from the Introduction and/or Big Picture 1 that you would like to discuss?

# THE HUMAN SCALE
## GREETING AND EATING

### The Power of Pressure

An experiment was once conducted at Princeton University on students of the theology faculty. Each was told to prepare a short talk. For half of the students the talk was to be on Jesus' parable of the Good Samaritan, and the parable was read out to them. Later each student was told individually to go to another room to record the talk. On the way to the recording room, each one passed a "victim" sitting slumped in a doorway, coughing and groaning. A note was made of those who stopped to ask if they could help and those who passed by.

Around half the students stopped, but it was not necessarily those who had just been thinking about the story of the Good Samaritan. What made the difference was not the Gospel story but two little words. To half the students in each set, after telling them to go to the recording room, the experimenter added testily, "Hurry up." Most of them obediently hurried and in their rush to prove themselves good students, chose to ignore the victim slumped in apparent pain.[8]

I suspect that most of you reading this have lives that are pressured in one way or another. Most of us rush through life barely stopping to look left or right, often so preoccupied that we don't even really see what's in front of us. If we were more attentive, we might discover just how powerful our tiny choices could be.

## The Power of a Gesture

Archbishop Desmond Tutu recounts a telling incident from his childhood in 1940s' South Africa. As a bare-foot ten-year-old, growing up in a slum area with dusty lanes and no sanitation, he was out one day with his mother when they passed a tall, gaunt, white man, wearing a flapping cassock and a big black hat. As he passed, the man raised his hat to Mrs. Tutu in greeting. The young Desmond was amazed—he had never before seen anything like it—a white man offering a courteous, respectful greeting to a black woman. It was a tiny gesture, but one Tutu never forgot.[9]

The white man was Trevor Huddleston, then parish priest of a black township in Johannesburg. Tutu went on to become the first black Archbishop of Cape Town and a key player in the battle against apartheid. That such a radical change could be achieved with so little bloodshed and revenge was due in great measure to his influence.

But perhaps it all began then with a spindly, bare-foot boy noting a tiny gesture. In a world where the white boys called taunts as he passed, where his father was regularly humiliated by demands to examine his "passbook," where black children scavenged for food in the dustbins of the white schools, Tutu began to believe that things could be different.

Of course there were many other influences. The missionary wife whom Tutu observed patiently teaching a blind, deaf, and dumb black man how to read and write in braille. The wise, black schoolmaster who taught him in a high school with not enough desks to go around. When as a teenager Tutu was immobilized in a TB sanatorium for nearly two years, Huddleston visited every week.

But I can't help thinking about that tiny gesture of the raised hat, and how very easy it would have been not to have done it. How very easy to have passed by without offering that gesture.

But Huddleston had learned to see people as people. "He made you feel special," said Tutu of him later. "He made you feel you mattered."

## The Power of a Purchase

Not long ago, banana farmer Deryk Smart was thinking of giving up. "If things don't improve, banana farming will be a dead industry," was how he saw the situation. Twenty-one-year-old Deryk, who farms on St. Vincent in the Windward Islands, is a dying breed. George de Freitas, who works for the local export company as well as running his own farm, sees the bigger picture: "Lots of young people have left. Farmers paint such a gloomy picture that youth don't want to get involved."[10] This might not matter so much if St. Vincent had any other industry. But it doesn't.

What's so strange is that, in the United Kingdom for example, people eat on average 22 pounds of bananas per person per year, contributing to a massive one billion dollar per annum industry. Someone's getting rich, but it definitely isn't the banana farmers. In the last few years prices have plummeted worldwide and banana growing, often on small family farms, is in crisis.

But things are improving—just a bit. In January of 2000 the first fair-trade bananas hit the U.K. scene, and George and Deryk are among those benefiting from the change. Not only do they get a slightly better and, equally importantly, non-fluctuating price, but their local areas are also paid a "social premium" for projects which benefit the community. In George's town they are planning to open a nursery school and are looking at improving roads. They're also benefiting from a reduction in the amount of pesticides and other harmful chemicals in the environment. Not least, they are challenging the stranglehold of the huge multinational companies, which keep prices so low.

It's hardly a miracle cure. Fair-trade bananas at the time of writing are only available in a few of the major supermarket chains in the United Kingdom. They only make up 0.2 percent of the total E.U. banana market. They still don't sell at all in the United States or Canada. George and Deryk's livelihoods are still teetering on the brink of survival. But it *is* a change. It *is* a beginning. The small choice of choosing one bunch of bananas rather than another has made a difference.

## The Power of a Believer

I don't just mean a Christian believer here, although in both the situations I've just mentioned, it is Christians who have been at the forefront of change. I mean people who believe, against all the odds, that things can be different. (Strange but true—it is possible to be a Christian believer and not be interested in changing anything.)

One of my examples (that of Desmond Tutu) is from the struggle for black emancipation—a battle that, in institutional terms at least, has by and large been won. (I know there is still much more to be done in terms of changing attitudes, but slavery, colonialism, apartheid, and segregation have gone, and there are at least some black people in high positions in almost every social situation.) It's a struggle that has taken at least 200 years and many thousands, perhaps millions, of determined campaigners. Later in this book I will mention a few more of them.

The other example of banana farming demonstrates the struggle against trade injustice and Third World poverty—and that's one that is barely beginning. It is one of the most important battles our generation has to fight and, in my opinion, maybe *the* most important. But when we see the overwhelming habits of materialism in Western society, when we look at the giant corporations with more financial clout than many small nations, when we see the vast problems of poverty and hunger and lack of education and the spread of AIDS—it seems almost impossible that any of us tiny little Davids with our slings and our stones could possibly change anything.

But, hey, you get the allusion: that's where being a believer comes in. The Bible is full of people who triumphed against all the odds. It's also full of reminders to care for the poor. If you took a pair of scissors and cut out all the references to riches and poverty, you'd have a Bible in tatters.[11]

The Bible is full of giant-killers such as David, because they didn't do it alone. God was with them giving them courage, strength, and good aim. (Although, as someone pointed out to me, "When it comes to Third World poverty, the need is so colossal that whatever you do you're bound to hit the target somewhere. Maybe David's secret was that when he looked at Goliath, he didn't say, 'He's so big, I'm terrified.' He said, 'He's so big, I can't miss.' "[12])

So as we make our tiny day-to-day choices—greeting a passerby or choosing a slightly more expensive bunch of bananas from the shelf—we can be pretty certain that somehow or somewhere we are scoring a bull's-eye of need. We can also be sure that God is willing us on. I can almost hear him cheering.

—

The fact is that whether you eat or drink—whatever you do—you should do all for the glory of God (1 Cor 10:31)

## Small Experiments for the Week

How aware are you of who you pass by? This week try to notice someone you pass by regularly and at least choose to give him or her a smile. Perhaps be really daring with a hello.

How aware are you of what you eat? This week why not experiment by actively choosing to cut out of your diet one item that is unhealthy, unethically produced, or not environmentally sound, and replacing it with something better?

# WEEK TWO

*Nobody makes a greater mistake*
*than he who does nothing*
*because he could only do a little.*
*The only thing necessary for the triumph of evil*
*is for good men to do nothing.*

— Edmund Burke

*Each of us has a theological work to do.*
*We may think we haven't, but we can't help it,*
*because every time we make a decision or refuse to make one,*
*we are showing whether we are with Jesus or against him.*
*We are saying something about what we think Christianity is.*

— Rosemary Haughton

# THE BIG PICTURE
## THE CHURCH: REPRESSIVE OR REDEMPTIVE?

If there are some people out there who think God is the enemy of choice, there are certainly plenty who believe the Church is.

Quoting Philip Pullman again:

> There are two great powers...and they've been fighting since time began. Every advance in human life, every scrap of knowledge and wisdom and decency has been torn by one side from the teeth of the other. Every little increase in human freedom has been fought over ferociously between those who want us to know more and be wiser and stronger, and those who want us to obey and be humble and submit.[1]

Ruta Skadi, one of Pullman's characters in *His Dark Materials,* has no doubt what side the Church is on:

> For all its history...it's tried to suppress and control every natural impulse. And when it can't control them, it cuts them out.... That is what the Church does, and every Church is the same: control, destroy, obliterate every good feeling.[2]

It's not just the Church that is so often described as full of control freaks, but organized religion in any form. Scientist Peter Atkins voices an increasingly popular view: "My suspicion is that religions get themselves invented in order to keep their priests in power....

I think religions have grown as an exercise in power and that's all."[3]

### Sin and Shame

If you want to get such people ranting about the Church, there are certain buzz words you *must* employ: *evil, guilt, sin, shame, remorse, repentance....* You can probably think of others.

The problem is that these words are pretty much essential to an understanding of Christianity. Unfortunately, they can be key to misunderstanding it as well.

Let's look at that old-fashioned word "sin." I've put it in quotes for a reason—that's the way you'll almost always find it written in contemporary news reports. A good example is a story I read not long ago on how Pauline Prescott, wife of Great Britain's Deputy Prime Minister John Prescott, had been reunited with the son she gave up for adoption forty-three years previously. It told of how as a sixteen-year-old she "endured the most humiliating time of her life" when she was sent away to have the child at a nursing home "visited by vicars who preached on 'sinful love.'"[4]

Now I don't want to belittle the ordeal of the teenage Pauline or pretend that conditions at St. Bridget's House of Mercy weren't grim by current standards. But there's something about those quotation marks that seems to suggest it was the vicars and their remarks on sin that were making it a grim experience.

Actually, it was society as a whole—not just the Church—that cast shame on single mothers for sexual activity outside of marriage. And not without reason. When places like St. Bridget's were founded, and for centuries before that, a baby born without a father to support it was quite likely to starve. The social structure simply wasn't strong enough to support single mothers. There had to be some sort of social penalty to act as a warning, and disgrace was the only one available. And while the Church may well have reinforced that disgrace, at least it did something positive for the teenage mothers and their offspring. Of course, by the 1950s such places were becoming outmoded, but they provided a merciful solution at a time when the alternatives were much, much grimmer.

"Sin" is not a word invented by vicars to cast shame on others' sexual shortcomings. It is a word used to describe any action likely to create bad outcomes, not least of which is separation from God. It might sound old-fashioned to some, but the concept still holds. Our choices have consequences and sometimes those consequences are damaging to ourselves and others.

## Remorse and Repentance

Archbishop of Canterbury Rowan Williams, in his book, *Lost Icons,* has a chapter entitled "Remorse," in which he explores the rise in our generation of "unaccountable behavior." He comments on how "public power—even in disgrace—means never having to say you're sorry," and on how the most that politicians can ever admit to is an "error of judgment." Even President Clinton's lechery in the Oval Office goes by the pseudonym of "inappropriate" behavior. People in the public field are now accountable only to the media—that means that "the losses that matter are losses to an image." It's all about how far an image can be eroded before the person has to go.[5]

Yes, "remorse" and "repentance" are well out of fashion, part of that same family of words as "sin" and "shame." They imply condemnation and the piling on of guilt. They carry allusions of control and power.

Williams believes that a society without remorse becomes distorted, obsessed with the importance of image. Well, he would, wouldn't he? some might say. He's an archbishop; perpetuating soul control is his business.

I'm not sure that Williams is such a typical establishment figure, but even those who think he is would have to admit that Jesus certainly wasn't. The first word of Jesus' ministry was "repent," and he went on to repeat the message over and over. But it clearly wasn't so he could reinforce his control over his listeners—he was a wandering preacher who might never meet them again. He had no organization to support, no political agenda to promote, and no financial overheads to feed. A message like that was much more likely to lead to his downfall—and it did.

I saw a program on TV yesterday about a beauty salon. There were people, men and women, having their hair straightened, their eyebrows shaped, their nails lengthened. One woman was having her hair dyed pink in imitation of her favorite pop star. She had decided to reinvent herself. It's relatively easy to reinvent your image. It's much harder to deal with what's inside.

The program moved on to show someone having colonic irrigation—it wasn't the best thing to watch as I had my supper. The person in question was delighted with the feeling of having had so much impurity, residues from years of unhealthy eating, sluiced away. I suspect that the whole point of repentance, as far as Jesus was concerned, was something like that—a sort of "irrigation of the soul." It was not intended to pile on guilt, but rather to drain it all away.

## Boundaries and Burdens

So how has the Church built up this reputation as a purveyor of guilt?

Human society cannot exist without boundaries to behavior. I read an article recently about Christiania, an anarchic hippie commune in Sweden. It began in 1971 with a passionate belief in no rules, but has gradually been amassing a bigger and bigger rulebook as time has gone by.[6]

In a society like the United Kingdom, where Christianity has been a state religion for at least 1,500 years, it is hardly surprising that the Church has taken on the mantle of guardian of morality for society at large.

(And, curiously, even in today's secular society, there are passionate antireligionists who believe it still should do so. "It's terribly important," says atheist Will Provine, "that religious people begin thinking about the foundations of ethics and meaning in life for non-believers as well as themselves."[7] There seems to me to be a strange double-think going on there but, that aside, if you believe society needs some sort of ethic basis, then who else is there to provide it?)

Most of us who chose the Christian path did so because of some yearning to be good, to live meaningful lives. And it is not surprising then that in response to that yearning the Church is full of challenges—exhortations meant to direct us toward that good and meaningful life we seek. It's just that challenges, piled on week after week, month after month, can eventually become self-defeating. They can become burdens rather than blessings. We are just as likely to sink under their weight as to spring into action.

## Conscience and Condemnation

I'm already aware of that tension as I write this course. I've suggested that it's good to greet strangers and shop responsibly. And I genuinely believe it. The trouble is, I know I don't always do it.

When I look at how I respond to challenges there seems to be a pattern, which, if I am not careful, can go something like this:

challenge—>conscience—>consternation—>condemnation.

Let me explain. I hear a challenge—*tell someone about Jesus; recycle your tin cans; campaign for trade justice*—and because I have a reasonably tender conscience, it is pricked. I agree: Yes, that's right. I should do that. But then consternation kicks in. Because I'm already trying to implement a whole load of other challenges I also agree with: *care for your aging parents; pray for half an hour a day; exercise regularly; give to Christian Aid; water your potted plants; pay your bills.* It all seems a bit overwhelming and I slump on the sofa, watch junk TV, and munch my way through a packet of chocolate cookies. And then I feel condemned.

I really did want to be better! I really did want to do all those things! But it all got a bit too much. If I'm not careful, I will begin to harden my conscience, to build a thick skin so that all those demands just glance off me and never pierce the surface.

In my better moments, though, I can see a more positive pattern at work. And that goes something like this:

challenge—>consideration—>consciousness (Counselor)—>choice.

That means that when I hear the challenge, I don't immediately think: *Yes, I ought to do that.* Instead, I consider it: *Yes, that's clearly a good thing, but is it for me now?* And so it enters my consciousness (which I suppose is not so different from my conscience, except that it feels a bit less emotive and guilt-ridden and a bit more under my own control). And it swills around there for a while along with all the other challenges. And while it's doing that, I'm also handing it over to the Counselor—the name Jesus gave to the Holy Spirit, whom he promised would "guide you into all the truth" (Jn 16:13). Other translations of the same title put it as the "Helper" or the "Comforter," and they're both good words. The point is, we're not in it alone.

And so after a while some challenges emerge, while others sink away. I make a choice, just one small choice: I wash out a can and put it aside in a box. And later I find the postcard I was exhorted to send to my local politician and take a few moments to fill it in and find a stamp. And probably then I feel a bit better and remember to water the potted plants. And I decide that there's no way I'm going to sustain a regime of going to the gym twice a week, or praying for half an hour a day. But I could walk to the station instead of driving, and I could try praying for ten minutes a day while I'm walking.

And some of these efforts may turn out to be one-timers, but some will become habits that now, as I look back, I realize have become ingrained. And from some of those small habits have come further, bigger steps. And looking back I can see how those choices have made my life better and more meaningful, and I hope, maybe, even done so for others.

## Equal and Empowered

One image of the Church is as an army—with all the regimentation that implies. Another is as a hospital—

closer to Jesus' teaching perhaps, but still with the suggestion of dependence and control.

Neither of those images is entirely bad. Most of us at one time or another need to be dependent on others; most of us might benefit now and then from being under an imposed regime. Indeed, for those whose only childhood experience is of weak or confused parenting, these types of Christian community may be a lifeline. Nevertheless, they might not be a healthy image for intelligent, emotionally stable adults.

Maybe that hippie commune would be a better one? It is, after all, how the Church first began. The only trouble is that such idealistic prototypes never seem to last long—in Jerusalem or in Sweden!

The best image I can come up with is of a group of travelers journeying together across an alien landscape. We have a commission in common, we are intent on a common destination, we have a map, and an occasional mobile phone link to an outside Advisor! All the rest though—since we don't know beforehand the landscape across which we travel—we need to work out as we go along. If we are to survive, we need to respect each other, to listen to each other's experience and field of expertise. We need to understand that different members travel at different paces, and that at times we need to relieve others of their burdens and let them travel unencumbered. Above all we need to acknowledge that there are times when even the best of us will lose our way.

It's a flawed metaphor, I know. Perhaps you can think of a better one. The point is this: the Church is meant to be a free and equal association of flawed human beings. Its leaders are meant to be servants. Its authority can only work if it comes from Someone beyond itself.

And however often and however badly it gets it wrong, I still passionately believe that the Church can be like this. I've had some bad experiences of Church, but I've had some exceptionally good ones too! Church at its best can be both liberating and empowering.

The Church is not *them*—it's *us*. It's up to us to make it what we want it to be!

—

Jesus answered, "Those who are well have no need of a physician, but those who are sick; I have come to call not the righteous but sinners to repentance" (Lk 5:32).

Then Jesus said to the Jews who had believed in him, "If you continue in my word, you are truly my disciples; and you will know the truth, and the truth will make you free.... Very truly, I tell you, everyone who commits sin is a slave to sin...if the Son makes you free, you will be free indeed" (Jn 8:31–32, 34, 36).

# GROUP SESSION
## THE CHOICE OF LIMITATION

*Opening*                                     *1–2 min.*

Reminder of ground rules (see page 33).

Has anyone got anything they would like to discuss from readings or further thoughts from the previous session? If so, slot in an appropriate time, probably near the end.

*Clip 1: Babette's Feast*              *4 min. 30 sec.*
*Introduction to sisters—their charitable works, turning down marriage.*

*Discuss*                                     *5–10 min.*

The two sisters lived an immensely limited lifestyle. Did they have any choice in the matter or was it chosen for them?

Do you think they were wasting their possibilities?

What limitations or losses might they have encountered if they had made different choices—to become an opera singer or to marry the dashing young officer?

What good things happened as a result of the choice they did take up?

*Brainstorm*                                   *3–5 min.*
List all the choices you have made, or are likely to make, that impose limitations on your life in some way.

*Discuss*

Is it possible to make any choice that doesn't also constrain you in one way or another?

Reader 1: Matthew 7:13–14                    *30 sec.*

> "Enter through the narrow gate; for the gate is wide and the road is easy that leads to destruction, and there are many who take it. For the gate is narrow and the road is hard that leads to life, and there are few who find it."

*Discuss*                                    *4–8 min.*

What sort of narrowness does Jesus mean here?

Is he implying that all Christians are to live in an identical, proscribed way, or that each of us has a particular path (a "destiny") that is God's will for us?

Does this mean that a vast area of life experiences is off-limits to Christians?

*Ponder and Share (optional)*                *3–5 min.*

Do you perceive the Christian path you have chosen as a "narrow road"? If so, does it seem the best possible path for you, or do you struggle with regrets or yearnings for other paths? Think for a moment and then share as you feel able.

*Clip 2: Shawshank Redemption*               *3 min.*

Andy's arrival at the prison in chains. "You eat when I say you eat..." "Put your trust in the Lord, your arse belongs to me." Nothing left but all the time in the world.

*Discuss*            *5–10 min.*

Andy has nothing left but all the time in the world. What does he have left though? What choices does he still have?

"Put your trust in the Lord, your arse belongs to me." Do any aspects of our lives belong to others? Or only if we allow it?

What limitations in your life are imposed upon you? And what or who imposes them?

Is it possible to live your life without limitations imposed by others?

*Brainstorm*            *3–5 min.*

List as many areas of behavior as possible that society places legally off-limits.

Then list any areas of behavior you believe are categorically off-limits for Christians.

Mark those in both lists in which you feel there may be exceptions or provisos.

Reader 2: Genesis 2:15–17; 3:1–11, 22
(Garden of Eden, eating fruit)      *3 min.*

> The Lord GOD took the man and put him in the garden of Eden to till it and keep it. And the Lord GOD commanded the man, "You may freely eat of every tree of the garden; but of the

tree of the knowledge of good and evil you shall not eat, for in the day that you eat of it you shall die."

Now the serpent was more crafty than any other wild animal that the Lord GOD had made. He said to the woman, "Did God say, 'You shall not eat from any tree in the garden?'" The woman said to the serpent, "We may eat of the fruit of the trees in the garden; but God said, 'You shall not eat of the fruit of the tree that is in the middle of the garden, nor shall you touch it, or you shall die.'" But the serpent said to the woman, "You will not die; for God knows that when you eat of it your eyes will be opened, and you will be like God, knowing good and evil." So when the woman saw that the tree was good for food, and that it was a delight to the eyes, and that the tree was to be desired to make one wise, she took of its fruit and ate; and she also gave some to her husband, who was with her, and he ate. Then the eyes of both were opened, and they knew that they were naked; and they sewed fig leaves together and made loin-cloths for themselves. They heard the sound of the LORD God walking in the garden at the time of the evening breeze, and the man and his wife hid themselves from the presence of the Lord GOD among the trees of the garden. But the Lord GOD called to the man, and said to him, "Where are you?" He said, "I heard the sound of you in the garden, and I was afraid, because I was naked; and

I hid myself." He said, "Who told you that you were naked? Have you eaten from the tree of which I commanded you not to eat?"...Then the Lord GOD said, "See, the man has become like one of us, knowing good and evil; and now, he might reach out his hand and take also from the tree of life, and eat, and live forever...."

*Discuss*                                    *10–15 min.*

There are many things that are difficult about this story (see pages 182ff., for further study), but focus for the moment on three things about being human that it does make clear:

- God made humans with the capacity for choice;
- God set limits on what is allowed;
- Wrong choices have consequences.

Do you see the limitations that God sets here as a demonstration of his authority, as a test for humans, or as provisions for their own safety?

What does the story say about the consequences of wrong choice?

What other choices could Adam and Eve have made in this situation?

*Meditation*                                 *5–7 min.*

*Silence (or perhaps music)*                 *1–2 min.*

Bring to God anything during this session that has caught your imagination, annoyed, irritated, or challenged you, or anything you would rather not think about.

Reader 3: Ancient wisdom in contemporary words: verses from the Book of Proverbs adapted from *The Message* paraphrase of the Bible.

> Trust God from the bottom of your heart;
>> don't try to figure everything out on your own.
>> Listen to God's voice in everything you do,
>>> everywhere you go;
>> he's the one who will keep you on track.

> The ways of right-living people glow with light;
>> the longer they live, the brighter they shine.
>> But the road of wrongdoing gets darker and
>>> darker —
>> travelers can't see a thing; they fall flat on their
>>> faces.

> Keep your eyes straight ahead;
>> ignore all sideshow distractions. Watch your
>>> step,
>> and the road will stretch out smooth before you.
>> Look neither right nor left;
>> leave evil in the dust.

>> It's a school of hard knocks for those who leave
>>> God's path,
>> a dead-end street for those who hate God's rules.
>> A simple life in the fear of God

is better than a rich life with a ton of headaches.
Better a bread crust shared in love
than a slab of prime rib served in hate.[8]

*Silence*                                    *20–30 sec.*

Reader 4: The unknown writer of the following quote
has discovered that limitations are not always what
they seem:

I asked for strength that I might achieve,
I was made weak that I might learn humbly to
    obey.

I asked for health that I might do great things,
I was given infirmity that I might do better things.

I asked for riches that I might be happy,
I was given poverty that I might be wise.

I asked for power that I might have the praise of
    men,
I was given weakness that I might feel the need of
    God.

I asked for all things that I might enjoy life,
I was given life that I might enjoy all things.

I got nothing that I had asked for
but everything that I had hoped for.

Almost despite myself my unspoken prayers were
    answered,
I am among all people most richly blessed.[9]

*Silence*                                    *20–30 sec.*

Reader 5: Prayer
> Lord, our guide and companion,
> give us grace to accept those decisions made by
>    others over which we have no control.
> Give us courage not to give away to others the
>    free choices you gave us to make,
> and, please, Lord, give us the wisdom to know
>    the difference.
> Help us to accept our limitations.
> Help us to see within them the opportunities
>    that you offer. Amen.

*Silence*                                    *20–30 sec.*

# THE HUMAN SCALE
## ENCOURAGING AND ENABLING

### Parent Power

I don't suppose you've ever heard of Leona McCauley, and I'm afraid I can't tell you that much about her other than that she was the daughter of former slaves, a single parent to two small children, and a teacher in a rural one-room schoolhouse in Alabama. I can also tell you that she was a devout Christian, a strict disciplinarian, and a fervent believer in the power of education.[10]

I think I'm even more safe in assuming that you won't have heard of Alice L. White. Daughter of rich parents in the northern United States, she chose to move to the South to found a school for poor black girls, the Montgomery Industrial School for Girls— "Miss White's School," as it was more commonly known. But sadly, although I imagine her story contained more than its share of struggle, loneliness, faith, courage, rejection, and dogged determination, as far as I know it has not been documented.

"What I learned best at Miss White's school," said one of her pupils later, "was that I was a person with dignity and self-respect, and I should not set my sights lower than anybody else just because I was black."

That same pupil was, in fact, Leona McCauley's daughter, who later wrote that her mother was her greatest inspiration, teaching her to believe in freedom and equality and *"to take advantage of opportunities, no matter how few they were."*

Despite a better education than most of her fellow Southern blacks, there were to be few opportunities for the young Rosa McCauley. She had to drop out of college to nurse her dying grandmother, she became a seamstress, and she eventually married a barber, Raymond Parks. Hers was a life hedged in by limitations, typified by the bus she rode to work every day where she had to sit in the "blacks only" section at the back.

And by now you may realize that you *have* heard of Rosa Parks because of a small choice she made on her way home from work on December 1, 1955—a choice that led to her being dubbed the "mother of the civil rights movement." Rosa Parks was sitting near the back of the bus that day, just at the front of the blacks only section. But the bus was full and when the driver noticed a white man standing, he ordered four blacks to move from that row of seats. Three others complied. Rosa Parks refused and was arrested.

It wasn't the first time Rosa had been true to what she believed in. She had been thrown off a bus twelve years previously by the same driver and forced to walk five miles home in the rain. She regularly chose to walk upstairs in public buildings rather than take elevators marked "blacks only," she went thirsty rather than drinking from the "coloreds only" drinking fountain, and over the years she and her husband had worked quietly in the background, doing what they could for the National Association for the Advancement of Colored People.

But this time, things changed. Within twenty-four hours of her arrest, a boycott of buses was announced for the day of her trial. When she was convicted and refused to pay the fine, several thousand protesters formed the Montgomery Improvement Association and the one-day boycott stretched to 382 days and 42,000 protesters, almost bankrupting Montgomery's bus company.

What began as a tiny split-second choice swelled to a huge movement across the United States that, fueled by the oratory of Martin Luther King, eventually wiped out the segregation laws forever.

But in looking at Rosa Parks' small choice, I became fascinated by those unsung heroines, Leona McCauley and Alice L. White, the mother and the teacher, whose hidden actions taught Rosa to believe in herself and to be ready to grasp what few opportunities life offered.

## Grey Power

"Nothing left but all the time in the world." For many people retirement comes like half a life sentence, a vast looming gulf of emptiness. It seemed it might be so for some local friends of mine, George and Margaret Young. After a lifetime as a vicar, it was a bout of ill health that caused George to retire somewhat suddenly. They moved from a busy suburban parish to a tiny house in a Surrey village and experienced what Margaret describes as "a terrible bereavement."

"We'd always been so busy and so involved with other people's lives. At first you think it's wonderful, you're going to read and you're going to do this and that. But after a few weeks I remember George sitting in the chair and saying, 'Is this it?' There's only so many books you can read, and although I love being a grandma, you need to have something else as well."

It wasn't long in coming. Margaret had for many years sold fair-traded goods within their local church. "I saw this report in the newspaper about a fellow who had set up this new company [Traidcraft] and wrote to him to find out more." It was just a small-scale thing, a sideline, and "we'd always lived in big vicarages so finding somewhere to store it was never an issue."

But when the Youngs moved, it suddenly became a problem. "We still had quite a bit of stock and now we had absolutely no space to put it. We either needed to get rid of it or find somewhere to store it. Very soon we saw a sign just a few yards up the village high street saying 'Units to let.' We went to investigate and decided to rent a tiny room in what had once been the dairy block of a large country house. That of course meant we had to get a whole lot more goods and really work hard at selling them in order to pay the rent, so we took the plunge and set ourselves up as a not-for-profit company. That first year seemed completely futile. We went to see everyone we could think of in the area and no one seemed interested. We sat in our tiny rented room waiting for customers and reading an awful lot more books! Anyway, we battled on and just about broke even that year, selling about $18,000 of goods. Now we're selling around $18,000 per month!"

"We're not setting the world on fire," says Margaret. "We just see ourselves as enablers, telling people about fair-trade issues and helping them to sell goods where otherwise they might never get started."

I was curious to know what got them interested in the first place. For George it was a visit to South America, seeing fledgling workshops set up and realizing the difficulties they faced. "It just became impossible to escape the broader implications of the Gospel—for economic life and business in general."

For Margaret it was "a nagging sense that we saw the problems but weren't doing anything about them.... We felt God had been good to us, but that all the time we were just asking blessings for ourselves without tackling the really big issues."

In the ten years that George and Margaret have been running their fair-trade business, they have sold nearly $740,000 worth of goods (without taking a penny for themselves). Maybe not setting the world on fire, but as lights in the darkness go, it's pretty effective.

### The Power of "What If?"

What if Margaret Young had read the newspaper article, turned the page, and forgotten it? What if Miss Alice L.

White had bowed to convention and never gone to the South to see if there was anything she could do there? What if Leona McCauley had been so exhausted at the end of a day's work that she never talked to her small daughter about things she believed in?

The "What if" question is a good servant but a bad master. It is one of the greatest helps ever in sparking off creative thinking and pushing us to venture in directions previously untried. But when it gets tied up with fear and regret, it starts to master us and tie us in knots. "What if I hadn't made this or that mistake?" "What if I take this path and it turns out wrong?"

We all miss opportunities all the time. We all make wrong choices sooner or later. We have to start from where we are. We have to build on the choices we have made, not wonder about the ones we have missed.

Philip Pullman in his *His Dark Materials* trilogy explores this idea: "When you choose one way out of many, all the ways you don't take are snuffed out like candles, as if they'd never existed. At the moment all Will's choices existed at once. But to keep them in existence meant doing nothing. He had to choose after all."[11] This is where the idea of being on God's narrow way becomes a comfort rather than a constraint. If God is guiding our path, then we can trust him for the choices we miss as well as the ones we make. We can trust him that if we make mistakes, then he will put us back on the route—not necessarily the road we would have been on, because we probably cannot retrace our steps. But we can be sure it will be the best one to take from here on in, and who knows, may even be better than the original plan.

I have a friend with one of those in-car route planners. You feed in where you're coming from and where you want to go and it plots the route. Then as you're traveling, it tells you, in an intensely irritating voice, "Turn left at next junction," "Left turn coming up," "Turn left now," etc. But this is what is really clever—if for whatever reason you fail to do so, it doesn't sulk or tell you to go back or babble on regardless. "Recalculating," it says, "recalculating." Because of some amazing satellite technology, it knows exactly where you are and so simply recalculates your route starting from where you now happen to be. Bearing in mind just how paltry this technology is in comparison to the mighty mind of God, it may help us understand how God's plan for us is not just one "miss it and you've blown it" route, but an infinite range of possibilities constantly interacting with the choices we make.

## The Power of Restlessness

There's a statement of the Apostle Paul's that I've always rather envied. It's that one about having "learned to be content with whatever I have" (Phil 4:11). I'm rather comforted that it is something "learned." The fact that it has been acquired on a long rollercoaster ride of experience rather than in a sudden zap from the Holy Spirit somehow makes it more real and possible to me. Nevertheless, these verses still seemed to convey a sort of calm that was far from my experience and a passivity that I was not sure I wanted.

It was then that I glanced back a few paragraphs and realized that Paul was not only far from passive, he was also far from calm: "Forgetting what lies behind and straining forward to what lies ahead, I press on toward the goal..." (Phil 3:13–14).

This is someone who is far from satisfied, someone *"straining," "pressing on."* If there is contentment, it is like that of a mountain climber who simply doesn't notice what the bivouac is like, because all he feels is the exhaustion of a good day's climbing, and all he sees is the summit ahead of him, closer now in the moonlight beyond the tent door.

And in a funny way, that made me feel better, because it told me that the Apostle Paul shared the same sort of restlessness I experience, and perhaps Leona McCauley and Alice L. White felt too, and probably George and Margaret still feel even though they could justifiably claim they'd earned a rest.

This is a strange idea: that God may actually intend us to be *both* restless *and* content, and it brings us, as so many things in religion do, to the idea of paradox. Paradox is what you get when you try to reconcile two things that seem both true and irreconcilably opposite. Paradox is about holding these two things in balance, letting them be *both/and* rather than *either/or*. Faith, it seems, is full of paradoxes. For example, already in this course we have encountered the ideas of being:

- *both* dependent on mercy *and* working out your own salvation;
- *both* humble *and* recognizing your dignity as a child of God;
- *both* aware of your sin *and* secure in being forgiven.

Perhaps then it is possible to be *both* content within our limitations *and* actively pushing against them, expanding the boundaries, playing the "What if?" game, along with its companion "Why not?"

In any and all circumstances I have learned the secret of being well-fed and of going hungry, of having plenty and of being in need. I can do all things through him who strengthens me (Phil 4:12–13).

## Small Experiment of the Week

Look around you to see if there is someone voiceless or powerless whom you encounter but rarely notice. Think of some way of offering a small encouragement and then give it to them.

## WEEK THREE

*We are not permitted to choose the frame of our destiny.*
*But what we put into it is ours.*

— Dag Hammarskjöld

*He is invited to do great things*
*who receives small things greatly.*

— Cassiodorus

# THE BIG PICTURE
## NURTURE: BLESSING OR BANE?

### Creating an Identity?

A couple of years ago I went on a weekend course at a retreat center. It was all about honest communication. It was an interesting weekend—somewhat wacky, but also very moving. One reason it was wacky was the person leading it. His name was Pierre Leclerc. He was charming and he led it very well, and despite a heavy French accent his English was perfect. Nevertheless, it soon became evident that one or two people were distinctly unhappy with him, and halfway through the course we discovered why. It transpired that Pierre Leclerc was actually plain Peter Carter from Nottingham (I've changed the names for obvious reasons).

He never liked himself as he was before, he said. He wanted to be different and, being a good actor, he had decided to recreate himself with a new persona. As you might imagine, this provoked something of a reaction, especially on a weekend devoted to people sharing honestly! But after quite a stormy session, surprisingly most of the group decided to accept Pierre. It began when one person said something like: "Well, I always feel like I'm playing a role."

And it turned out to be a positive breakthrough for the group as a whole as others joined in with things like:

"I'm always trying to please people by being how they want me to be."

"Most of the time I feel I'm wearing a mask."

"No one knows the real me."

My first reaction was that yes, my colleagues were right. We all portray ourselves, in one way or another, as we want others to see us, and therefore who am I to judge? But I've thought about it a lot since then, and now I'm not so sure.

It's not that I think changing your name is necessarily a bad thing. I have a friend who was christened Fifi. Now that may have been an appropriate name when she was a cute little girl, but by the time she was a forty-year-old woman and larger than average in both directions, it was very inappropriate indeed. It took her until then to change it, and she probably should have done it years earlier. Her confidence certainly seemed to blossom when she did.

And since this year I've managed to shed forty-two pounds, change my tortoiseshell-framed glasses for some rimless ones, and have my hair streaked red. You can see that I'm not necessarily against someone changing their image.

But the more I've thought about it, the less I've become convinced about the Pierre Leclerc phenomenon. He was, he claimed, trying to become more truly who he believed himself to be. The trouble was that he wasn't just giving himself a new name or a new image, but also a new history. The new persona he had taken on was actually a total denial of his roots.

Of all the many choices we do have, the raw material we have to work with is not one of them. We come ready-made with a certain physiognomy, a certain family, a certain community, a certain cultural heritage. And those things we cannot change.

Rowan Williams points out that "No one at all 'decides their fate' in the sense that their choices shape *only* their lives and possibilities, or that *only* their choices shape their lives and possibilities."[1] We are all shaped by the choices of millions of others before us, not least the choice of our parents to copulate at a specific moment in time! And we in our turn, perhaps in every single tiny choice we make, are shaping the world for others.

As we look at this idea of small choices, we have to do it in the full understanding not only that every choice we make impacts on others around us, but also that however much we try, we cannot shape our world by our choices alone. We are impacted irrevocably and constantly by the choices of others.

It's an ongoing process but, of course, it is especially true of childhood.

## Connecting Pathways

Professor Robert Winston explains that our personalities are formed at the very smallest level, in the 100 billion neurons that make up our brain. As children develop, these tiny neurons, or brain cells, are sprouting more and more branches to make connections with one another. At the same time, however, almost as quickly, other branches and their connections are being pruned. This constant growth and pruning in children's brains is being shaped all the time by what's happening to them and how they react to it all. Specific experiences in childhood are beginning to develop specific characteristics in our brain, and it is in this way that different aspects of our personality are developing throughout our childhood. Winston pictures it as rather like walking through a field of wheat:

> When children have a new experience, whether good or bad, the neurons make new connections. These connections cause pathways and it's these which affect the way children behave not only now, but also later in life. In the beginning they're hardly there, just like the trail we leave in a field of wheat for the very first time. But if as children we have the same experience several times, our behavior begins to form a pattern, and the pathways in our brain become better established. It's rather like treading the same path several times.
>
> So if we repeat an experience over and over and over again, we're laying ever clearer routes through our brain, until finally we've created the equivalent of an expressway. The new aspect of our personality has formed. The characteristics we develop in childhood are most likely to stay with us for the rest of our life.[2]

So we can never totally erase our history. It is written at the most basic level of our beings. All is not lost, however, as Winston affirms:

> The brain is the most remarkable organ in the body because it can transform itself. We can use our minds to improve and transform our minds, something that

no other animal can do. In the case of personality it means we can become a little more like the person we would like to be.[3]

## Creating a New Way

Robert Winston is affirming what the first chapters of Genesis assert. There is something uniquely different about human beings. We have some astonishing capacities, foremost perhaps our capacity for language. But there are two others that are vital to remember when we seem bound by the heritage of our past:

- creativity: the capacity to make something new and exciting from the materials God has given;

- imagination: the capacity to envisage something hitherto unseen.

Being made in the image of the creator God means that we have an amazing capacity not only to imagine something original and unique, but also to bring it into being. It's true that some other creatures could be said to make things, as in birds making nests and spiders spinning webs, but there still is a huge qualitative difference in what humans can achieve. We are the only creatures that seem able to go on, generation after generation, bringing into being things that have never been before.

This doesn't mean that change for change's sake is always advisable. *If it ain't broke, don't fix it.* There is something wonderful in being rooted in a tradition, and something tragic in sweeping it all away.

## Changing from the Inside Out

But if we do see the need for change within ourselves, how can we do it? How can we change those neurological pathways that have been set invisibly inside us? It seems we can change some patterns by willpower and choice. Others, though, seem much too deeply ingrained.

Carl Jung, in his pioneering work in psychology, pondered how God might fit in: "If there is a God, the ground of being, it does not seem inconceivable that he might find in this archetypal world of the unconscious his point of individual interaction with us."[4] The Bible, of course, uses the "heart," rather than the "unconscious," as an expression of the deepest part of our personality. But its writers had no doubt that it is a place where God can work. The psalms are full of this understanding, and the Prophet Ezekiel too voiced this willingness of God to transform from the inside out: "I will give them one heart, and put a new spirit within them; I will remove the heart of stone from their flesh and give them a heart of flesh" (Ezek 11:19).

It's interesting to note that the Bible has several examples of people being given a new name:

> God said to him, "No longer shall your name be Abram, but your name shall be Abraham; for I have made you the ancestor of a multitude of nations" (Gen 17:3, 5).

> Then the man said, "You shall no longer be called Jacob, but Israel, for you have striven with God and with humans, and have prevailed" (Gen 32:28).

> And Jesus answered him, "Blessed are you, Simon, son of Jonah! ...And I tell you, you are Peter, and on this rock I will build my church..." (Mt 16:17–18).

These renamings were not artificial reinventions. They were not pretending these people had come from different origins than they really had. They signified a change that was already happening and it was happening from the inside out. They were public expressions that Abraham, Jacob, and Simon had potential they had not reached yet. As they lived their lives with God they had the possibility of being different. But it was a difference that would come from within—from following, from obedience, and even from a spiritual wrestling match.

## Cutting Apron Strings

Jesus seems to have a very odd and ambivalent attitude to parents. He makes it quite clear very early on in the Sermon on the Mount that he has not come to abolish the Law (cf. Mt 5:17)—a Law that states quite clearly in the Ten Commandments: "Honor your father and your mother" (Ex 20:12). In fact, later he strongly criticizes those who use religion as an excuse not to honor and help their parents, claiming that "So, for the sake of your tradition, you make void the word of God" (Mt 15:6).

But then we have this terribly disturbing passage in Matthew 10, where he says that he has actually come to turn people against their parents. He cannot be clearer: "Whoever loves father or mother more than me is not worthy of me" (Mt 10:37).

And then there is the incident when Jesus is speaking to a crowd and someone tells him that his mother and brothers are there. Jesus, claiming that his disciples are now to take the place of his family, apparently disowns them: "Who is my mother, and who are my brothers?" (Mt 12:48) And yet, at the end, during his torment on the cross, he takes the trouble to ensure that his mother is both cared for and given another focus for her own caring: "Woman, here is your son" (Jn 19:26).

How does all this add up? Well, we can certainly conclude that:

- we are to love God above all else;
- we are to treat our parents with respect;
- we are to ensure they are provided for.

But in another of those paradoxes, I think we can also conclude that Jesus not only gave his followers permission to cut loose from their parents, he was actually telling them to do so.

The Bible commands that we are to honor and respect what shaped us, but it clearly shows that we are not intended to be limited by it. What was good for one generation is not always right for another. There may be many things we need to shake off or at least re-examine. (You may have heard the old anecdote about the woman who, when preparing her Sunday roast beef, always cut off each end and put it sideways in the tin. When asked why, she explained it was the way her mother had always done it. But one day she finally got round to asking her mother the reason. The answer was simple: "Because I only had a small roasting pan and it wouldn't fit otherwise.")

Not everything our parents, our upbringing, and our cultural heritage land us with is good or appropriate for now. Sometimes we need to ask ourselves what we have taken for granted and whether it still applies.

Science shows us a natural world constantly evolving and full of possibilities for change. It seems obvious that God intended the same for human society. The whole point of the endless roll of generations is that children, rather than simply carrying on what has gone before, are free to envisage and put into practice a new way of being. We are formed by the choices of our parenting, but we are not to be tied by them.

This is what the Lord says...
> "Do not remember the former things,
> or consider the things of old.
> I am about to do a new thing;
> now it springs forth, do you not perceive it?" (Is 43:18–19)

# GROUP SESSION
## THE CHOICE OF IMAGINATION

**Welcome**
Reiterate ground rules if necessary
(see page 33).                                    *2 min.*

Is there anything from the latest readings which you would like to comment on or discuss? (Save long issues and try to fit them in later in the session.)

**Introduction**
So far we've looked at:

*Observation*—the need to be fully aware of the present moment in order to notice opportunities for choice.

*Limitation*—looking at how choice always takes place within a framework, either chosen by us or imposed on us, and how no limitation is so tight as to eliminate choice totally.

Now we're going on to:

*Imagination*—the importance of taking a creative leap beyond that which we already know.

**Clip 1: Shawshank Redemption**                *7 min.*
*Andy gets delivery of books—plays Mozart—hope is a dangerous thing.*

*Brainstorm*                                    *6–8 min.*

What choices did Andy make here? What other choices can you remember from the rest of the film? Try to notice how one choice led to another.

*Discuss*                                      *8–15 min.*

Why did Andy choose to act the way he did?

What effect did hearing Mozart have on the prisoners and why?

All of us need moments of transcendence—like "some beautiful bird flapping into our drab little cage"—moments that make us aware of something beyond our narrow horizons. Is it possible to choose to create such moments and, if so, how?

*Ponder and Share*                             *8–15 min.*

What made Andy different was that he saw possibilities and was ready to seize the moment of opportunity. We are back to the power of observation. Can you think of any examples in your experience when, by creative thinking or seizing a moment, you or someone else has been able to make a difference?

Reader 1: Matthew 25:14–19, 24–30          *1 min.*

"For it is as if a man, going on a journey, summoned his slaves and entrusted his property to them; to one he gave five talents, to another two, to another one, to each according to his ability. Then he went away. The one who had received the five talents went off at once and traded with them and made five more talents. In the same way, the one who had the two talents made two more talents. But the one who had received the one talent went off and dug a hole in the ground and hid his master's money. After a long time the master of those slaves came and settled accounts with them.... Then the one who had received the one talent also came forward, saying, 'Master, I knew that you were a harsh man, reaping where you did not sow, and gathering where you did not scatter seed; so I was afraid, and I went and hid your talent in the ground. Here you have what is yours.' But his master replied, 'You wicked and lazy slave. You knew, did you, that I reap where I did not sow, and gather where I did not scatter? Then you ought to have invested my money with the bankers, and on my return I would have received what was my own with interest. So take the talent from him, and give it to the one with the ten talents. For to all those who have, more will be given, and they will have an abundance; but from those who have nothing, even what they will have will be taken away. As for this worthless slave, throw him into the outer darkness, where there will be weeping and gnashing of teeth.' "

*Discuss*                                    *10–15 min.*

What do you need to "have" in this context in order to be given more?

Is there such a thing as a no-talent person?

What stopped the one-talent guy from using what he had been given?

***Clip 2: Babette's Feast***                                    *3 min.*
*Babette tells about money all spent—"Give me the chance to do my best."*

***Discuss***                                                   *1 min.*
Babette's feast was a huge extravagant act. Do you see her extravagance as a virtue or a folly?

Reader 2: Matthew 26:6–13                        *1 min.*

> Now while Jesus was at Bethany in the house of Simon the leper, a woman came to him with an alabaster jar of very costly ointment, and she poured it on his head as he sat at the table. But when the disciples saw it, they were angry and said, "Why this waste? For this ointment could have been sold for a large sum, and the money given to the poor." But Jesus, aware of this, said to them, "Why do you trouble this woman? She has performed a good service for me. For you always have the poor with you, but you will not always have me. By pouring this ointment on my body she has prepared me for burial. Truly I tell you, wherever this good news is proclaimed in the whole world, what she has done will be told in remembrance of her."

*Discuss* **3–5 min.**

You could consider the woman's act to be as wasteful as the burying of the talent, if not more so. What is the difference and why did Jesus condemn the one and praise the other?

*Options* **5–10 min.**

Brainstorm 1

Can you think of any other extravagant or risky acts in the Gospels or in the Bible as a whole?

and/or

Brainstorm 2

Both Andy and Babette knew that there was a price to be paid for their actions, but they were willing to pay it. Think of as many examples as you can, from your own experience or from your knowledge of the world and its history, where the price of a creative act has been high, but ultimately worthwhile.

*Meditation* **5–7 min.**

*Silence* **2–3 min.**

To ponder: It's not only artists who want the chance to do their best. What would you like the chance to do your best in?

What small thing could you do to make the world a better place?

Reader 3: A meditation from Charles Péguy, nine-teenth-century French Catholic writer, entitled "God's Dream":

> The Lord God said:
>> I myself will dream a dream within you,
>> good dreaming comes from me you know.
>> My dreams seem impossible, not too practical
>> nor for the cautious man or woman;
>> a little risky sometimes, a trifle brash perhaps.
>> Some of my friends prefer to rest more com-
>>     fortably
>> in sounder sleep with visionless eyes.
>> But from those who share my dreams I ask
>> a little patience,
>> a little humor,
>> some small courage,
>> and a listening heart—
>> I will do the rest.
>> Then they will risk and wonder at their daring;
>> run, and marvel at their speed;
>> build, and stand in awe at the beauty of their
>>     building.
>> You will meet me often as you work
>> in your companions who share the risk,
>> in your friends who believe in you enough
>> to lend their own dreams, their own hands,
>> their own hearts, to your building.
>> In the people who will stand in your doorway,
>>     stay awhile

and walk away knowing that they too can find
   a dream.
There will be sun-filled days
and sometimes a little rain—a little variety
both come from me.
So come now, be content.
It is my dream you dream,
my house you build,
my caring you witness;
my love you share,
and this is the heart of the matter.[5]

*Music*                                           *2–3 min.*

Reader 4: Prayer
Read aloud together as a benediction for one another:

> May the God of hope fill each of us with all joy
> and peace as we trust in him, so that each of
> us may overflow with hope by the power of
> the Holy Spirit.[6]

# THE HUMAN SCALE
## CAMPAIGNS AND COMMUNITY

I've discovered a curious fact. As soon as you start to talk about creativity, there will always be someone who says, "Not me, I haven't got any imagination. Not a creative bone in my body, I'm afraid." What they usually mean is, "I can't paint or write or perform on a stage," or, "I'm just ordinary, not one of those dynamic gifted types." Or, in other words (returning to Jesus' parable in Matthew 25), "I'm just a one-talent person, I'm afraid."

But creativity is about a lot more than the traditional artistic gifts and it's not just limited to a few particularly gifted individuals. In fact, it flowers best when practiced by a group of ordinary people who care about something and get together to laugh and argue and spur each other on. Just to prove it, I want to tell you about a few creative actions by ordinary people that I've discovered recently by opening the pages of my newspaper, and about one that I've experienced firsthand.

### Campaigning for Justice

The first news report[7] that took my eye was focusing on a creative bit of activism by a group drawn together from local churches, temples, mosques, charities, and trade unions in London's East End. TELCO, The East London Communities Organization, decided it was time to highlight the huge gulf between rich and poor not somewhere out there in the Third World, but the gulf right there where they lived, in the U.K.'s capital city.

East London is a microcosm of contrasts. On the one hand, shabby streets and grim public housing; on the other, the gleaming towers of Canary Wharf, moated and security-guarded like a fortress. By day Fortress Canary is home to thousands of highly paid workers in the finance and media industries. But as evening falls and they depart for their leafy suburbs, a new workforce takes the night shift, an army of contract cleaners, local people about whom the regular employees are blissfully unaware.

TELCO decided they ought to know, and so it was that at the Annual General Meeting of HSBC, one of Canary Wharf's (and indeed the whole U.K.'s) largest companies, one Abdul Durrant bravely stood up to address the assembled shareholders to ask them how they thought they would manage raising a family in London on $9 per hour.

There was a certain amount of coughing and shuffling, but Sir John Bond, executive chairman, on a salary of 3.44 million dollars, agreed to meet Durrant and other local representatives. He thought he had an answer, listening politely, then reeling off a list of local charities supported by HSBC. "Sir John," one of them explained, "you don't understand. We're not asking for charity. We want justice."

TELCO's creative idea? Nothing complicated, nothing clever—simply buying some shares for a contract cleaner so that he could have his say.

## Crusading Online

Campaigning on local issues is relatively easy, but how do you change something halfway around the world?

Another article caught my attention recently when it spoke of "digital missionaries" and villagers in Laos accessing the Internet via "pedal-power."[8]

It has long been recognized that information is power, and one of the greatest gaps between the powerful and the powerless arises as a result of the availability of access to information technology, or the lack of it. Two people whose creative thinking managed to shift the power balance a little are Lee Thorn and Bounthanh Phommasathit. Thorn is a U.S. Navy veteran who once bombed the village in which Bounthanh's family lived. The organization they founded together[9] began with a need for reconciliation and drew together Laotians, Lao-Americans, and war veterans. But soon they were asking themselves what they could practically do together. And it became clear again that what local people most wanted was not just charity but justice—and in particular the chance to get a fairer price for their crops.

The rice farmers of Phon Kham village live in a remote mountain region where monsoons often cut off road access and electricity, and phone networks are nonexistent. The only knowledge they had of the price of their crop was from the man who came to buy it. They had no idea of market prices and so, as Thorn explains, "They were consistently being ripped off. They needed communications to give them more economic power."

But it wasn't just a case of buying a computer, a generator, and a stationary bike to power it. In an area of torrential rains followed by high temperatures and thick red dust, standard technologies just wouldn't function. And so the organization created a tough dust- and water-proof computer using off-the-shelf components and low levels of electricity. They believe they have now created a potential tool for the rural poor in locations all over the world.

It's true that some of that creativity came from leading computer designers who were persuaded to give their time for free. But the first steps came from two people who believed in reconciliation and wanted to show it. The second steps came in gathering a team of others who shared their concerns, and the third in discussing and carefully listening to what the people on the ground had to say. Once these steps had been put in place, the imaginative leap toward a revolutionary new solution was relatively easy.

## Combating Mediocrity

Creative campaigning doesn't always need to be about blatant injustice. Sometimes it just needs to highlight the terrible downward slide into mediocrity, which a worldview that only recognizes financial values seems naturally to create.

The Italians know a thing or two about lifestyle, so perhaps it's not surprising that two recent initiatives to halt declining standards have begun there.

The first was provoked when McDonalds opened a fast-food restaurant by the Spanish Steps in Rome. A Piedmontese journalist was incensed when he heard the news and so the Slow Food Movement[10] was born. It champions the "right to taste" (something of which Babette would surely have approved) and promotes healthy eating and environmentally sound farming, not to mention the delights of regional specialties and the survival of small-scale food producers.

From its humble beginnings in 1986 as a local gathering in a small town in the Piedmont region, the Slow Food Movement has now spread to eighty-three countries and has more than 60,000 members.

The second creative campaign involves a protest about Italy's dire television programming. (Having recently visited Rome and spent several late nights in a dreary hotel room flipping through forty channels of dross, I can affirm that they really do have something to complain about.) This time the news article I discovered[11] told of a viewers' strike involving an estimated 400,000 people who decided to turn off their TV and do something more interesting. "We want to say to people that there are better ways of spending their free time than to stay at home staring at television," proclaimed a spokeswoman for the protesters, whose slogan is "Television Is Nasty and Bad."

The creative idea here was again a simple one—persuading companies and organizations to offer discounts or free entry to anyone who turned up clutching *"il telecommando"*—the humble TV remote control. The idea snowballed and soon there was a nationwide network of museums, heritage sites, clubs, theaters, cinemas, and restaurants all offering perks and discounts to anyone with a TV zapper in their hands.

Since Italy's prime minister at the time of writing is Silvio Berlusconi, a man whose family owns 95 percent of all Italy's broadcast media, it seems doubtful that the campaign will have much immediate impact. But as one of Rome's newspapers commented, "Sometimes ideas turn out to be worth much more than their immediate value." Who can tell what vast changes in society come from small actions or words that somehow touch a nerve?

## Community Building

My last example is not such an exciting story, I'll admit. In fact, it's one that's all too familiar to many churchgoers—about how our local congregation raised funds to build a new church hall.

We did all the usual things, of course. We prayed, we had a gift day for church members, we baked cakes, we sold "bricks" around the village, we appealed to the local council. All these things played their part, but it was far from being enough. So we started on events—a concert, a murder mystery evening, a quiz night, a wine tasting, a silent auction—and a rather noisier one! We got on to sponsoring. Some noble soul had his hair, beard, and eyebrows shaved off. The vicar, being a water-sports enthusiast, did a sponsored canoe trip down the Thames.

Others, quite outside the church, heard of our efforts. One local farmer offered a field full of Christmas trees if we were ready to chop them down and sell them. Another local, a retired artist, offered some paintings she no longer had room for. It seemed like a well-intentioned though not particularly valuable offer, until we discovered that she had for many years been an illustrator for a top greeting card manufacturer and had over 500 original paintings to dispose of. When someone, he of the regrown hair and eyebrows, decided to do some determined selling all over the county, the paintings quickly raised over $37,000!

Meanwhile, in the background, one quiet salt-of-the-earth pensioner had been writing endless letters and filling in endless forms to grant-making trusts, and eventually a few of them came up trumps.

And at last, between all these varied activities—and with the constant underpinning of prayer—we made it. The money came in and the hall was built.

I know it's not that unusual or remarkable, but when I look back, it fills me with pride because I see such a diverse bunch of people bringing their skills, their determination, and their imagination together to create something that will serve our local community for generations to come.

## Coming Together

There is another reason besides pride though, which prompts me to mention our church hall. It's because it's a prime example of something experts tell us is fast becoming endangered and liable to face extinction. It's something called *social capital*.[12]

It seems that our governments in the wealthy West and those that advise them have suddenly woken up to the fact that a nation's wealth does not lie only in its financial capital. Nor does it lie only in what is termed "intellectual capital"—education and earning power—nor just in industry or infrastructure. It lies in something much less tangible; something which is slipping away fast—by fifty percent over the last four generations, in fact.

Social capital can loosely be described as anything that bonds people to work and interact together within a community. It is "the glue which holds societies together."

So the very ordinary things that happen in our new church hall—Sunday morning children's groups, Line Dancing, Over-60s Keep Fit, Victim Support Group, Mothers and Toddlers, Choral Society, Brownies, Youth Group, Women's Breakfasts, etc.—are prime examples of social capital and a vital contribution to the wealth of the nation.

But membership of voluntary groups and community activities have declined drastically in recent years. Generation by generation there is less and less. (It is true that membership of organizations like Amnesty or Greenpeace is up, but in these terms membership mainly means receiving a newsletter. There is no face-to-face meeting and that, in terms of social capital, is what matters.)

Of that fifty percent drop, it is reckoned that ten percent can be put down to pressure in time and money, and another ten percent to what can be described as suburbanization: the fact that so many of us commute long distances to work and live in urban sprawls with no clear geographic identity. A massive twenty-five percent is put down to the all-pervasiveness of electronic media: TV, computers, walkmans, etc. Margaret Thatcher famously proclaimed that there was no such thing as society, and maybe it was a self-fulfilling prophecy.

But why does all this eager joining of groups and getting together matter so much?

Perhaps the most important word to sum it up is *trust*. Not the sort of deep trust that evolves within marriage or long-term friendships, but the general level of mutual trust that comes about when people belong to some organization or other, when they regularly turn up, do their bit, learn to cooperate and work together and make things happen. Trust has been described as "society's oil can." The engine dies without it.

It is easy to see the effects of this erosion of trust. It is there in the rise of the litigation culture: if you think you have grounds to sue someone, then why not do it? You can see it in the spread of bureaucracy: the increased demand, especially for public-sector workers, not just to do their job, but to keep detailed accounts of every moment of it. And you can see it in surveys: in the United Kingdom and the United States, around eighty percent of those over seventy believe their neighbors can be trusted. When you ask sixteen- to twenty-nine-year-olds, the figure drops to less than forty percent. As to the percentage who trust politicians, priests, or almost anyone in authority, the numbers are almost sliding down the scale.

You can see it too in the breakdown of the nuclear and the extended family. You can see it in employment patterns—the old idea of a lifetime's employment in one company has long gone. Whether these are causes or effects is arguable, but the result is summed up in the words of a father: "When I talk to my kids about loyalty and commitment, they just laugh, because there is nothing in their experience that measures to that."

"The key to reversing the decline in social capital," says bishop of Maidstone, Graham Cray, "is people whose character makes them trustworthy." And character like that is something that is grown. It is formed by the decisions we make in relationship with others. We can change—by the choices we make, by the small steps we take into community and commitment—into people who are worthy of trust.

The Church of Jesus Christ, far from being an outmoded anachronism, is a key resource in contemporary society. It is a guardian of social capital, a production plant in faithfulness.

—

Jesus said to him, "If you are able!—All things can be done for the one who believes" (Mk 9:23).

Jesus looked at them and said, "For mortals it is impossible, but not for God; for God all things are possible" (Mk 10:27).

## Small Experiment of the Week

What might you do that would brighten the lives of others you live or work among? Find a friend or colleague and toss ideas around—as wacky or unusual as you like—until you've thought of some small creative and original act that is possible to implement. Then decide how and when you will do it, preferably together.

# WEEK FOUR

*It is better to begin from one's feeble state*
*and end up strong,*
*to progress from small things to big,*
*than to set your heart from the very first*
*on the perfect way of life,*
*only to have to abandon it later.*

— Evagrius of Pontus

*Lord, help me to begin to begin.*

— George Whitfield

# THE BIG PICTURE
## NATURE: SERVANT OR MASTER?

I've touched on the idea of evolution already in this book, but now the time has come to take the plunge and delve more deeply into the questions about choice and freedom that it offers.

The reason I wanted to take this foolhardy leap can perhaps be summed up best by the following quote from biologist and atheist Will Provine:

> If evolution is true, then none of the things that deeply religious people want to be true are in fact true. No God. No life after death. No free will. No ultimate meaning in life and no ultimate foundation for ethics...an evolutionary explanation is just incompatible with a Christian...or any other kind of view that suggests purposive forces guide the process producing the organisms we see now.[1]

Over the years I've occasionally stumbled across such statements—on TV, radio, in magazines—and although everything in my gut has told me they can't be right, somewhere a nagging question remained. Could that be true? Is it really a logical conclusion?

On and off over the years, I've pursued the question and I'm glad to say that in the end my head has joined my guts in emphatically refuting it.

This may not be an issue that bothers you and, if so, feel free to skip this chapter. (I'm aware that for some tastes it will be rather heavy, and for others irritatingly simplistic!) Whatever you do though, please pause to read the wonderful affirmation in the Bible verses at the chapter's end!

## The Ongoing Creation

The response to statements like Provine's in some sectors of the Church has been to retrench into aggressive creationism.

For myself, I had been comfortably ignorant on the issue for most of my life until about twelve years ago when I was asked to ghost-write for someone who held creationist views. It happened that at the time we had a friend living with us, an up-and-coming expert on biodiversity, who gently pooh-poohed the evidence I was trying to rewrite and carefully explained why. It was a difficult time for me, but I read and thought and eventually decided I couldn't in all conscience write what I didn't believe. I declined the commission.

This is not the time or place to wade deeply into the issues that led me to that view, but it seems to me that if you put the mechanics of evolution alongside a belief in a Creator who chose that mechanism, then together they have something astonishing to say not only about the way in which small "choices" have the power to affect big changes, but also about the way in which God interacts with his world.

It's not just my idea that the two might actually fit together. Ecologist Sam Berry believes that Darwin's theories, far from being evidence against God, actually fit together a scientific observation of nature and the biblical idea of God more fully than before:

> Darwin destroyed the possibility of the viewpoint that God, having created the world and made it perfect, then retired above the bright blue sky. If there was going to be a viable belief, then God had to be *in* life, holding together life, acting through normal processes. In theological language, God was immanent as well as transcendent. So Darwin, in a sense, brought the two [science and religion] together.[2]

In other words, if you believe that creation is something that happened right at the beginning of time, with everything set to a perfection (which humans then spoiled), then it is very easy to conclude that the Creator might have just withdrawn and let us get on with it. But if you believe that creation itself is an ongoing process, then it has powerful implications about the way God works.

John Habgood, archbishop of York and also a scientist, explains it thus:

> God is involved in a continuous process of which we are a part. The very method of creation almost allows things to make themselves, to develop themselves with a great degree of openness. This speaks to me of a God who wants to create a universe, which in some sense is allowed to be itself.[3]

So the kind of God that Jesus came to show us, a Father intimately involved with his creatures, yet allowing them freedom to be themselves and to make choices about how they live, suddenly makes sense in a new and exciting way.

It so happened that at the end of my time of struggle twelve years ago, we went to spend Christmas with relatives in Arizona. And who would go to Arizona without visiting the Grand Canyon? I remember standing on the South Rim and being blown away not just by its immensity and beauty (for which no photo can ever quite prepare you), but by the immensity of the God who created it. I was seeing the handiwork of a Creator who was prepared to do his work step by step, layer by layer over time beyond my comprehension. What I was looking at was evidence of an incredibly *patient* God.

The excitement of that discovery has stayed with me down the years. If God is that patient with lumps of rock, then he is surely just as patient with us, his children. And if he can bring that much beauty out of layers of dust, detritus, and decay, out of volcanoes and fault lines and the constant wearing down of running water, how much more can he work creatively with us, with our choices, and even with our mistakes?

## The Selfish Gene

But this argument, of course, depends on the possibility of us having free choice. And some would argue that contemporary science proves we don't. Will Provine again: "Humans are comprised only of heredity and environment, both of which are deterministic.... So from my perspective as a naturalist, there's not even a possibility that human beings have free will."[4] Provine acknowledges that humans do go through decision-making processes, but asserts that it is only in the same way as a computer plays chess. We only decide what we are already programmed to decide.

And what is doing the programming? Our genes, of course. We are, in this worldview, no more than temporary host environments, being manipulated by and for the real power behind the throne—our selfish genes.

It is Richard Dawkins who has popularized the idea of the selfish gene. Whereas human lives are fleeting, it is genes, he asserts, that are the immortals: "It [a gene] leaps from body to body down the generations, manipulating body after body in its own way and for its own ends, abandoning a succession of mortal bodies before they sink in senility and death."[5]

And genes, says Dawkins, are essentially selfish, their only purpose being to ensure their own survival:

> The predominant quality to be expected in a gene is ruthless selfishness. This gene selfishness will usually give rise to selfishness in individual behavior.... Much as we might wish to believe otherwise, universal love and the welfare of the species as a whole are concepts that simply do not make evolutionary sense.[6]

It is the gene that in Dawkins' view is "the fundamental unit, the prime mover of all life." Humans are no more than convenient survival machines, programmed with an urge to procreate so the gene can never die.

There is a problem with this view, however, that a few wise commentators have been quick to spot. Philosopher of religion Keith Ward explains:

> It is distinctly odd to say that what an engineer might aim for is the emergence of programs for building bodies, while the actual existence of the bodies themselves is an irrelevant by-product. It is just like saying that the important goal of cookery is the production of recipes. The cakes themselves are unintended by-products of the recipes.[7]

## The Disturbing Conclusion

And there is another problem which Dawkins himself points out. It is all very well to assert that this "survival of the fittest" is the mechanism by which nature works, but it is a very dangerous model to apply to human society. Dawkins, while describing himself as "passionately Darwinian" as a scientist, acknowledges that he is "passionately anti-Darwinian when it comes to politics and how we should conduct our human affairs."

> I am not advocating a morality based on evolution...I am not saying how we humans ought to behave. My own feeling is that a human society based on the gene's law of universal ruthless selfishness would be a very nasty society in which to live.[8]

There is ample evidence for this conclusion. Take "survival of the fittest" as a model for society to its logical conclusions and you arrive, as many respected and respectable people did at the beginning of the twentieth century, at the idea of eugenics, the possibility of breeding a master race. Take that to its political conclusions and you quickly arrive at something like the Holocaust. Take "survival of the fittest" to its economic conclusions and you arrive at a belief in the all-pervading power of a market economy. Combine this with radical globalization—the belief that there should be no restrictions on the power of multinational companies—and it is arguable, to my eyes at least, that in the long term this may prove almost as damaging to society as a whole as the worst madnesses of Hitler.

But if the genes are in control, do we even have a choice? Will Provine believes not:

> There is no ultimate responsibility that can be laid at the feet of human beings. One can be conditioned or trained or educated to be morally responsible, and I believe that moral responsibility is essential to enable us to live together in society. But that's programmed into us by others around us, by cultural traditions and so on. There's no hint, to my mind, that the moral responsibility exhibited by human beings comes from any freedom of the will.[9]

I'm not sure where an atheist like Provine believes that moral responsibility ultimately comes from, or how he accounts for us being educated or trained unless others choose to do so, but I can see some logic in his conclusions.

Dawkins, however, despite his view that "the historical process that caused you to exist is wasteful, cruel, and low,"[10] struggles to assert a view of humanity as capable of higher things: "One unique feature of man...is his capacity for conscious foresight.... It is possible that yet another unique quality of man is a capacity for genuine, disinterested, true altruism. I hope so...."[11] But if the power that made us is simply our selfish genes, then it must be at best a very faint hope.

## The Limits of Science

Perhaps Dawkins' problem is that outlined by linguist and renowned thinker Noam Chomsky: "As soon as questions of will or decision or choice of action arise human science is at a loss."[12] Evolution may explain the mechanism by which we became what we are, but it breaks down when it tries to explain meaning. It shows us how the computer works, but it fails to explain who programmed the computer and, more importantly, why.

Bring God into the picture and it begins to make a little more sense.

Scripture asserts that our world is not fundamentally ruthless and cruel and low, but fundamentally good. It asserts that the unique qualities of human beings are far more than just lucky happenstance. It asserts that there is a God, a being of supreme goodness and beauty, who deliberately chose to make humans in his own image.

Scripture is realistic, though, acknowledging right from the beginning that human life is not all sweetness and light. It acknowledges that there are powerful drives within us and that those drives tend always to selfishness and that, left to their own devices, they do indeed make for "a very nasty society in which to live."

## The Ongoing Struggle

Paul, that great popularizer of Christian ideas, had a problem:

> I do not understand my own actions. For I do not do what I want, but I do the very thing I hate.... For I do not do the good I want, but the evil I do not want is what I do (Rom 7:15, 19).

And curiously, although he labels this drive as coming from "sin" rather than selfish genes, he also describes it as something "living in me."

He knows there is something higher that he wants to attain to, but he sees this drive as a natural law—what he describes as *"the law of sin and death."*

I don't mean to say that we can use the idea of genes, even selfish ones, as an exact equivalent of sin. Our genetic inheritance has given us many good things, not least the instinct for survival. But however you define it, there is undoubtedly some selfish pull inside humanity that leads, if unchecked, to a society spiraling downward into something nasty and cruel. And however much we would like to think it was just "them" causing these problems, in truth we know that the tendency is also there in us.

"Who will rescue me from this body of death?" asks Paul in a cry of desperation.

From Richard Dawkins' viewpoint, there is only one way. We have to do it ourselves: "If, as my wife suggests to me, selfish genes are Frankensteins and all life their monster, it is only we who can complete the fable by turning against our creators."[13] The only way out of this "nasty, cruel, and low" process, according to Dawkins, is through defiance against everything that has made us what we are.

But how could we, if we were no more than hosts for our selfish genes, possibly pull ourselves up by our own bootstraps? Thankfully Scripture has another answer. The story of the Gospel is that we are not bound by our genetic programming. There is a possibility of choice and change. The Gospel tells of a different possibility, one in which the Creator is working with us right from the start. Paul works through his despair to a final triumphant conclusion. We are not in it alone. Rescue is possible "because through Christ Jesus the law of the Spirit of life set me free from the law of sin and death."

---

...With the Lord one day is like a thousand years, and a thousand years are like one day. The Lord is not slow about his promise, as some think of slowness, but is patient with you, not wanting any to perish, but all to come to repentance (2 Pt 3:8–9).

# GROUP SESSION
## THE CHOICE OF DETERMINATION

*Introduction*                                        *1 min.*

So far in the sessions we have looked at how good choices involve:

*Observation*—the need to be fully aware of the present moment to notice when opportunities present themselves.

*Limitation*—all choice takes place within a limited framework; every choice we make means ruling out other possible choices; no situation is so limited as to prevent choice.

*Imagination*—to choose creatively means taking an imaginative leap beyond what is familiar and safe.

Our next vital ingredient for choice is:

*Determination*—there are plenty of people and circumstances ready to block our good choices; how can we overcome them?

*Clip 1: Shawshank Redemption*                        *9 min.*
*Andy's escape.*

*Discuss*                                        *10–15 min.*

What does that final image remind you of? Do you suppose it was intentional?

The film's title speaks of redemption. How was redemption played out in the movie and who was redeemed?

Andy's understanding of geology—that anything could happen given enough pressure and time—gave him the patience to do something remarkable. Has our modern world conditioned us into being too impatient and, if so, how?

Should we resist this conditioning and, if so, how?

***Ponder and Share***                           *5–10 min.*

Previously in the film we saw how Andy's persistence in sending a letter a week for six years finally paid off. If you were to write a letter a week about something you really cared about, what would it be and why? Think for a moment and then share.

***Brainstorm***                                 *8–12 min.*

List as many advancements or benefits to society that you can think of (present day or throughout history) that have come about because of the persistence of an individual or a group.

Reader 1: Luke 11:5–10                           *1 min.*

> And he said to them, "Suppose one of you has a friend, and you go to him at midnight and say to him, 'Friend, lend me three loaves of bread; for a friend of mine has arrived, and I have nothing to set before him.' And he answers from within, 'Do not bother me; the door has already been locked, and my children are with me in bed; I cannot get up and give you anything.' I tell you, even though

he will not get up and give him anything because he is his friend, at least because of his persistence he will get up and give him whatever he needs. So I say to you, Ask, and it will be given you; search, and you will find; knock, and the door will be opened for you. For everyone who asks receives, and everyone who searches finds, and for everyone who knocks, the door will be opened."

### *Ponder and Share*                                   *10–15 min.*

What is it that stops you being persistent, either in prayer or in action? What discouragements have there been that made you give up on a particular aim or objective?

Have you had experiences where you have given up, but then decided to pick yourself up and persevere? What was it that motivated you not to give up?

### *Clip 2: Babette's Feast*                                   *3 min.*
*Anecdotes about the pastor and the chef at Café Anglais.*

### *Discuss*                                   *10–15 min.*

Both the pastor and the chef were inspiring people whom others admired. Why?

Both required a degree of single-mindedness to become who they were. What are the necessary ingredients of single-mindedness?

Andy and Babette each took a risk in their choices —Andy risked death or even longer imprisonment; in making the feast, Babette took a risk that it would not be appreciated or that the sisters might not continue to care for her. Would their choices still have been worthwhile even if they had failed?

***Optional extra***                                              *4 min.*
Christians have been known to take bold risks, but they have also taken very stupid ones, often on the grounds of "The Lord told me...." Is it possible to take risks without being irresponsible? If so, how?

***Meditation***                                                  *4–6 min.*

***Silence***                                           *30 sec.–1 min.*

Reader 2: Matthew 17:20                                    *15 sec.*

> He said to them, "For truly I tell you, if you have faith the size of a mustard seed, you will say to this mountain, 'Move from here to there,' and it will move; and nothing will be impossible for you."

***Silence***                                           *30 sec.–1 min.*
To ponder: nothing seemed more impossible in the first century A.D. than that a mountain might move. We now know that they are moving all the time—thrusting up, sinking down, shifting across continents—but slowly, very slowly. Strip this passage of any assumptions about sudden, dramatic miracles and see what it says about the power of human choice.

Reader 3: An extract from Nelson Mandela's inaugural speech in 1994:

Our deepest fear is not that we are inadequate.

Our deepest fear is that we are powerful beyond measure.

It is our light, not our darkness that frightens us.

We ask ourselves:

Who am I to be brilliant, gorgeous, talented, and fabulous?

Actually, who are you not to be?

You are a child of God.

Your playing small doesn't serve the world.

There's nothing enlightened about shrinking

so that other people won't feel insecure around you.

We were born to manifest the glory of God that is within us.

It's not just in some of us.

It's in everyone!

And as we let our own light shine,

we unconsciously give other people permission to do the same.

As we are liberated from our own fear,

our presence automatically liberates others!

*Silence*                                              *1–2 min.*

Reader 4: Prayer

God of power and might,

help us to take your long view and not our own impatient one.

Give us the persistence and single-mindedness
    to pursue the dreams you give us.
Show us how to believe in ourselves,
remind us of the immense power that rests in
    human hands.
Show us how to believe in your power,
remind us that even the largest mountains
    move, almost inevitably, given time.
Teach us always to ask you for what we need,
and to act not just out of our own strength and
    understanding, but from yours.
Amen.

# THE HUMAN SCALE
## SMALL STEPS AND LONG JOURNEYS

Hidden away along an insignificant footpath, at a place where the London suburbs finally give way to country-side, is a place I visit when I feel in need of inspiration. It's called Wilberforce's Oak; it's not on any tourist trail and, with only the smallest of signposts to guide you there, is easily missed.

If you do get there, you will discover that the oak itself is no more than a withered stump. You will find yourself above a steep descent into a wooded valley, with little to see but treetops, perhaps a spiral of wood smoke and a few passing airplanes. The only thing to mark the place is a seat with a plaque attached that tells you that here in 1787 William Wilberforce resolved to devote himself to the abolition of the slave trade.

I stumbled on Wilberforce's Oak by accident, and it might have been no more than a pleasant place to pause on summer evenings had I not discovered that the Abolition of Slave Trade Act was not actually passed until 1807. Twenty years.

Twenty years it took from that moment of decision to the point where the deed was accomplished, and it is this that prompts me to use Wilberforce's Oak as a small place of pilgrimage whenever I feel my hopes and dreams are too long in being fulfilled or I am too small for a task ahead.

I wonder if Wilberforce himself returned there when his hope was low. Certainly there were times when his resolve wavered and he was close to giving up.

## Time and Pressure

Wilberforce was twenty-eight when that first decision was made, and no newcomer to politics—he had already been a Member of Parliament for an amazing seven years. Even so it was perhaps with the blithe confidence of youth that he wrote to a colleague, "assure yourself that there is no doubt of our success."[14]

Within two months of that letter, he was cast down into the deepest despair. An illness (probably ulcerative colitis, a stress-related condition) brought him close to death and the prescribed cure of opium (a common one in those days) did little to help his emotional state. "Corrupt imaginations are perpetually arising in my mind and innumerable fears close me in on every side," he recorded in his notebook.[15]

For by then he was beginning to realize the strength of the opposition. Those he thought supporters were stalling and turning away, friendships were beginning to be broken, there were threats of physical assault.

Nevertheless, in 1789 Wilberforce addressed Parliament on the issue, in a passionate three-and-a-half-hour speech. Evidence was brought for both sides, but delay followed delay and the opposition, with its strong financial leverage, gathered momentum. In 1791 the motion was defeated by 163 to 88.

Every year thereafter, Wilberforce brought the issue to Parliament. He campaigned up and down the country, working on many other important matters in the meantime, but never giving up that which lay dearest to his heart. In 1807 he was finally successful.

You might think that after twenty years, he was able to rejoice in his triumph, but it was not so. For even then it was only the slave *trade* that Parliament abolished. It was, as Wilberforce well knew, only the opening salvo in a long battle. The actual ownership of slaves continued in Britain's colonies exactly as before, and there were plenty of other nations happy to go on trading. So Wilberforce kept on. "I am quite sick of the wear and tear of the House of Commons and the envy, malice, and all uncharitableness," he wrote in 1820,[16] but he would not allow himself to retire, still feeling the burden of failure. "Alas, alas, how grieved I am that I have not brought forward the state of the West Indian slaves."[17]

His sense of guilt and disappointment grew and his health, never good, began to fail. He knew his end was near. It was just three days before his death when he finally heard that the Bill for the Abolition of Slavery had been passed by the House of Commons.

## One Small Prayer and Two Open Hearts

Thirty or so years ago, a young couple, Mick and Angela Prentice, was feeling disappointed and disillusioned. Mick had believed he was called to become an Anglican vicar, but after a two-year process he had been turned down. A response of anger might have been understandable, but instead Mick and Angela knelt by their bed and prayed a simple prayer: "Use us, Lord, in whatever way you want."

Today 290 children in a shantytown in Kenya are receiving an education they wouldn't have had were it not for Mick and Angela. And that's beside the 134 British children who have found a loving foster home with the couple—some just for a night or so, but others for fourteen years.

The fostering was the first result of that prayer. It was when their own children kept laying an extra place at table by mistake that they wondered if God might be telling them something, and they decided they had the space to take in another child. The fostering grew until it became a full-time job for both Mick and Angela, although without a full-time wage. "We lived by faith for ten years. It was amazing how our needs were provided for. And how, when the need stopped, the money stopped."

That, you would have thought, was a big enough answered prayer. But through it Mick and Angela had learned to open their hearts and their purses to God and there was more to come.

The next adventure began in 1993 when the tax department gave them an unexpected rebate and they decided to use it on the holiday of a lifetime in Kenya. They flew to Mombasa and from there embarked on all the usual tourist excursions. Each time the journey involved traveling from Mombasa, an island, to the mainland via the Likoni ferry, and each time they were appalled to see children, some as young as seven or eight, begging on the ferry or sleeping in the dust at the port.

And the holiday was developing another dimension. On the first night at the hotel there had been a reception for guests, and the hotel manager, a young woman named Judith, had surprised them by coming up and asking if they were Christians. "I promise you, we weren't displaying any obvious signs," says Mick. The young woman explained that she hated these socials and had just been praying that she would meet some Christians. Over the week they got to know her better, taking up her invitation to go to a prayer meeting in a nearby township, and discovered her anxieties over her son, whose only chance for education was at a Moslem school with strong indoctrination into Islam. At the end of the holiday they gave Judith all their remaining money for her son to be educated at a Christian establishment.

They returned home and thought that was that. But Angela couldn't get the image of those children begging out of her mind. She wrote to Judith and asked if there was any charity they could support to help those children get an education. There wasn't, Judith replied, but she did know a Baptist pastor who was hoping to set up a school. They corresponded with the pastor and discovered that he had recently been called by God in a dream to move from his up-country home to a place called Shonda, somewhere he had never heard of before. He found it on a map, traveled there, and began a church meeting under a tree. Some Canadians had helped provide a church building, and now he was hoping to begin a school. Mick and Angela sent him some money and thought that was the end of it. But six months later the pastor wrote saying he had now begun the school, meeting in the church building, but needed more funds. Mick and Angela talked to their vicar, who wisely suggested that they shouldn't send any more money until they were sure how it had been spent. So Mick and Angela set out again for Kenya. On their arrival in Shonda, they found thirty-five children lined up to greet them with a song of welcome.

## A Step Forward and a Snowball Effect

At this point, says Angela, "We knew it wasn't going to go away. We either stepped forward or said, 'Very nice, thank you, goodbye.'"

"So we stepped forward. We met the children and the teachers and had the most wonderful week exploring possibilities, but we had no idea how we were going to do it. But we came home and started to fundraise between family and friends, sharing the story between our church and some other local churches. And the money started to come in, and soon we were able to build two classrooms."

Angela, a teacher, also took the story of Shonda to St. John's, her local primary school. Since the school at Shonda had also been named St. John's, the children's curiosity and then concern was aroused, and the link between the two schools became firmly established. They even have a school uniform in common. Parents in the United Kingdom began to pass on used uniforms; now some even buy two sets, one for their own child and another for a child in Shonda. The children raised money to enable the village to dig a well, so they were no longer dependent on buying bottled water. They had a book sale and raised money for the Shonda school to start a library.

Meanwhile, the whole thing had begun to snowball as adults caught the vision and began to sponsor a child or the school as a whole. There is plenty more of the story to tell, but the result is that the Shonda Project is now a registered U.K. charity[18] with a busy committee of fundraising volunteers, and St. John's First Baptist School in Shonda now has eight classrooms, thirteen teachers, and 290 pupils, and has just completed a workshop for secondary and adult vocational training. It receives no help from its own government or from other sources.

## Humble Beginnings and Huge Consequences

Mick and Angela decided early on that it was important for them to visit Shonda annually to keep track of where the money was going, and over the years they have taken many people with them. (Everyone, Mick and

Angela included, pay their own fares and stay at local hotels rather than take from the villagers. They visit the school and help in the classrooms but don't do building work because that too would take away from local people.) "It's changed our lives," says Angela, "and everyone who goes says the same. They all come back a different person." "The amazing thing," says Mick, "is that over there they've got so little, but they've got so much faith. That's what motivates us. Over here we've got so much, but we've got so little faith."

Mick and Angela don't see themselves as special people. Their actions have gathered them no fame. I only know of them because they live nearby and a mutual friend insisted I would be interested in their story. As Angela showed me her photo albums—eager rows of uniformed children, breeze-block schoolrooms, netball matches, science experiments, endless beaming smiles—her pride was mixed with amazement. "I still can't believe it."

Mick summed it up: "It's been incredible. It just has to be God in the center of this. It's not what we've done, because we're not that sort of people. We're of very humble background. To think that I'd ever be involved in setting up an educational establishment—my schooling was almost nonexistent!"

## Big Toe and Bathplug

Mick and Angela began with a small prayer of willingness and absolutely no idea where it would lead.

Wilberforce, standing under his oak tree, must have had some idea of the vastness of the issue, but even then no inkling of the personal cost that would last a lifetime. Would any of them have begun if they had known the enormity of the task ahead?

Would any of us have made the big life decisions—pursuing further education, marriage, parenting, moving somewhere new, pursuing a career—if we knew the hard times we might meet?

Thankfully we don't know, and when we do meet the difficulties, like Mick and Angela and William Wilberforce, we find God gives strength we never knew we had. The important part is beginning.

Some years ago I learned a valuable lesson. It involved a big toe and a bathplug. We were living in a community household at the time and, besides having two lively young sons and the complications of sharing space with another family, there were several needy people in residence. Our bedroom was also used as a writing space for myself and a mini-recording studio for my husband—and the situation was straining our relationship close to the breaking point. The only place where I could truly have a safe space to myself was the bathroom. So I got in the habit of retreating to soak in a hot bath whenever the pressure got too much.

But the really difficult thing was getting out of that bath. I lay there, warm, secure, and alone, and even though I knew there were a dozen things outside needing my attention, I simply didn't have the emotional energy to move. I just couldn't make myself get out of that bath.

So I devised a strategy. What I could do, I discovered, was to hook my big toe around the chain attached to the bathplug. Just the tiniest of movements and the plug came out. Then I either had to sit up to replace it or lie there and watch the water drain away. Either way it worked. If I sat up, then I had moved and I might as well get out anyway. If I lay there, within a few minutes I was shivering and forced to find a towel!

Very often the most difficult choice any of us has to make is simply that of overcoming inertia. It is the choice to move rather than remain static, to step out into the cold rather than remain in the safety of a warm, private cocoon.

At the risk of mixing metaphors, here's something else I learned a long time ago. It's a small saying, origin unknown: "A becalmed ship can't be steered."

In other words, if we're stationary, it's hard for God to lead us anywhere. If we're moving (with good intent), then even if it's the wrong way, it becomes much easier for God to point us in the direction that is best.

—

> Commit your way to the LORD;
>     trust in him, and he will act.
>     He will make your vindication shine
>         like the light,

and the justice of your cause like the noonday...
Our steps are made firm by the LORD,
When he delights in our way;
though we stumble, we shall not fall headlong,
for the LORD holds us by the hand (Ps 37:5–6,
    23–4).

## Small Experiment of the Week

Where is the inertia in your life? And what is the dream?
Decide on one tiny step to get yourself moving in the
right direction. Then do it. Commit the rest to God.

*For the want of a nail, the shoe was lost.*
*For the want of a shoe, the horse was lost.*
*For the want of a horse, the rider was lost.*
*For the want of a rider, the battle was lost.*
*For the want of the battle, the kingdom was lost.*
*And all for the want of a horseshoe nail.*

— Old proverb

*True spirituality is an exquisite awareness*
*of the connectedness of all things.*

— Tom Mahon

# THE BIG PICTURE
## CHAOS: CHANCE AND CONNECTEDNESS

Back in Isaac Newton's day, science was all about discovering fixed laws. It was the most logical place to start. If scientists could see a phenomenon that seemed to be predictable—the path of the planets, the apple falling—they could try to understand why and how. The laws they discovered in those simpler days still hold good. Gravity still keeps us from floating away. The galaxies still choreograph their way across the heavens. The area of a circle still equals $\pi r^2$. The angle of incidence still equals the angle of reflection. We live in a universe that runs within a basic ordered framework.

It was Darwin, of course, who first upset the scientific applecart. Not only did he challenge the assumption that the earth came into being settled and sealed in seven days, even more worrying was that little word "random," which had begun to creep in.

It was not going to go away.

As science marched on, it began to explore things way beyond what could be perceived in everyday life. Microscopic particles, time measured in millionths of seconds, distance in light years. And it discovered that at these far reaches things were rather different.

Einstein was the next to complicate things, suggesting that time and space were not fixed in their relationship to each other. Past, present, and future were rather more blurred than we thought.

Then Heisenberg, he of the Uncertainty Principle, made it all even more surprising by discovering that at the subatomic level all matter is subject to unpredictable fluctuations. Microscopic events occur in what seems a random way. The nuclei of radioactive atoms suddenly decay "just like that."

More recently came Chaos Theory: the whole universe, it turns out, is just like a teenager's bedroom. Well no, not exactly—rather, that even within a universe that obeys fundamental physical laws, there is disorder, complexity, and unpredictability.

The familiar concept, quoted with many variations is that "when a butterfly flaps its wings in Beijing, it can set off a tornado over Texas."[1] In other words, tiny variations in initial conditions can lead surprisingly quickly to huge changes in patterns of weather, ecosystems, stock markets, civilizations—in fact, almost anything.

We always knew that, of course. It's just that, since there was no way of understanding these things, science quietly put them to one side. The advent of breathtaking computer power changed all that. Suddenly it was possible to perform hundreds of millions of complicated calculations in a matter of seconds. And so it became possible to look more closely at those events that seem completely unpredictable and random—the "perfect storm" that hit North America's eastern seaboard in October 1991, why VHS took off as a video standard rather than Betamax, the spread of Aids, the 1929 stock market collapse, the global phenomenon of Harry Potter.

Useful lessons have been learned—patterns have been discerned, influencing factors have begun to be grasped. But one lesson has rung out loud and clear: "there are inherent limits to our understanding."[2] There are some things we never can predict.

It's not so much that things are inherently messy, more that they are inherently sensitive to the slightest tiny change. It's as if life is on a knife-edge, so finely balanced that at any time things could come down either way.

## A Step off the Path

The science fiction writer Ray Bradbury has written a short story on this theme, about a group of time travelers who are transported back to prehistoric times. As they arrive, they are told that they must keep strictly to the path—one constructed to float six inches above the earth's surface so that it will touch nothing. The expedition's leader, Travis, explains why:

> "Say we accidentally kill one mouse here. That means all the future families of this one particular mouse are destroyed, right?... And all the families of the families of that one mouse! With a stamp of your foot, you annihilate first one, then a dozen, then a thousand, then a million, billion possible mice!"
>
> "So they're dead," said Eckels. "So what?"
>
> "So what?" Travis snorted quietly. "Well, what about the foxes that'll need those mice to survive. For want of ten mice, a fox dies. For want of ten

foxes, a lion starves. For want of a lion, all manner of insects, vultures, infinite billions of life forms are thrown into chaos and destruction. Eventually it all boils down to this: fifty-nine million years later, a caveman, one of a dozen on the entire world, goes hunting wild boar or saber-toothed tiger for food. But you, friend, have stepped on all the tigers in that region. By stepping on one single mouse. So the caveman starves. And the caveman, please note, is not just any expendable man, no! He is an entire future nation. From his loins would have sprung ten sons. From their loins one hundred sons, and thus onward to a civilization. Destroy this one man and you destroy a race, a people, an entire history of life.... Perhaps Rome never rises on its seven hills. Perhaps Europe is forever a dark forest, and only Asia waxes healthy and teeming.... Queen Elizabeth might never be born. Washington might not cross the Delaware, there might never be a United States at all. So be careful. Stay on the Path. Never step off!"[3]

Lest any reader is now feeling guilt pangs because they once trod on a mouse or swatted a fly, remember that scientific research has proved the remarkable capacity of ecosystems to recover after some disaster seems set to destroy them. But of course it does happen: species are snuffed out forever. Fertile forests do become deserts. Civilizations do fall. And we cannot get away from the fact—sometimes they do so as a consequence of tiny human actions.

## A Chance to Do My Best

Einstein was famously skeptical of the science that came after him. His oft-quoted cry of "God does not play dice"[4] was not an affirmation of his belief in a loving Father, but a protest at the latest theories of quantum physics, which suggested that at the subatomic level there were mysterious random uncertainties at work.

But what if God does play dice?

What if God has chosen chance as one of his mechanisms? What if he wants us to have a chance meeting here, a haphazard train of thought there, an accidental discovery somewhere else? What if God puts those things in our path—like the legendary apple falling on Newton's head, or Alexander Fleming happening to notice mold growing on an abandoned laboratory dish? What if things happen randomly not because there is no meaning, but because there is?

For without randomness, what opportunities would there be? If things always ran on set paths, how many possibilities would disappear?

"Give me a chance to do my best," cries Babette, to explain why her feast is so important to her. The word "chance" and the word "opportunity" are interchangeable.

There is another word that comes to mind. It is serendipity—"the faculty of making *happy chance finds.*" I have a feeling that God is in the business of serendipity; that he delights in letting happy chances come our way—precisely because he delights in us. I think it is what Scripture means when it promises: "We know that all things work together for good for those who love God..." (Rom 8:28).

The verse has an interesting rider, sometimes forgotten: "those...who have been called according to his purpose." Perhaps God's serendipity is not just for us to enjoy, but also to fulfill the purpose to which he has called us?

## A Chaotic Sort of Order

And perhaps chaos is not as fearful as it appears, but something to be rejoiced in. For one of the conclusions of chaos theorists is that the connections between chaos and order are closer than was ever thought possible.

It seems that, to have the sort of order that flows organically, rather than being constrained and regulated, you first need a degree of chaos. Belgian chemist Ilya Prigogine wrote a famous book called *Order out of Chaos* in which he explained how it is only from systems that are "far from equilibrium" (in other words, in such a state of disorder and change that they can never settle back to what they were) that new order emerges.

I'm beginning to sense a lesson emerging here for today's Church. Fewer priests, reconfigured parishes, charismatic gifts, contemporary language, even which group's donations are accepted—the capacity of the Christian faith for disorder and dispute seems limitless. But what if they are an inevitable part of God's plan to bring something new and better? When things are in disarray and it seems they can never go back to the way they were, it scares us. But maybe it shouldn't.

Prigogine wrote of his conviction that irreversible chaos had a constructive role: "It makes form. It makes human beings."[5]

## A Butterfly Flap of Prayer

I am not the first person who has wondered whether this idea of the flap of a butterfly's wing might have spiritual implications. Novelist Susan Howatch, in explaining why she donated a million pounds to set up a chair of science and religion at Cambridge University, asked, "Might not people praying together be the equivalent of a butterfly's wings?"[6] Why shouldn't the same mechanism that allows tiny fluctuations to effect big changes in the physical world be at work in the spiritual realm as well?

Whether such things could ever be scientifically proven is another question. I believe in prayer and practice it, albeit falteringly. I'd certainly affirm that my praying changes me. I'd go beyond that, too. There have often been times when the old saying: "when I pray the coincidences start happening..." has proved itself true. But further than that I cannot go. I can't prove to you that my prayers for earthquake victims in Iran or political prisoners in Burma are having any direct effect. And maybe neither I nor anyone else ever will be able to.

In Bradbury's short story, the time traveler goes on to modify his dramatic theory about the mouse:

"Of course maybe our theory is wrong. Maybe Time can't be changed by us. Or maybe it can be changed only in little subtle ways. A dead mouse here makes an insect imbalance there, a population disproportion later, a bad harvest further on, a depression, mass starvation, and finally a change in social temperament in far-flung countries. Something much more subtle like that. Perhaps only a soft breath, a whisper, a hair, a pollen on the air, such a slight, slight change that unless you looked close you wouldn't see it. Who knows. Who can really say he knows? We don't know. We're guessing. But until we do know for certain whether our messing around in Time can make a big roar or a little rustle in history, we're being careful...."[7]

I cannot know for certain what consequences my prayers and actions may have. But since I don't, I have chosen to "stay on the Path." I am basing my choices on something I can't prove. Having faith, in other words.

—

For my thoughts are not your thoughts,
    nor are your ways my ways, says the LORD.
    For as the heavens are higher than the earth,
    so are my ways higher than your ways
    and my thoughts than your thoughts.
    For as the rain and the snow come down from
        heaven,
    and do not return there until they have watered
        the earth,

making it bring forth and sprout,
giving seed to the sower and bread to the eater,
so shall my word be that goes out from my
    mouth;
it shall not return to me empty,
but it shall accomplish that which I purpose,
and succeed in the thing for which I sent it
    (Is 55:8–11).

# GROUP SESSION
## THE CHOICE OF AFFIRMATION

### Introduction
So far, we've been talking about the necessary ingredients to make good choices—observation, limitation, imagination, determination—as attitudes that we need to adopt. This session changes tack with a look at how we deal with wrong choice and how sometimes the most basic ingredient for good choice may need to come from outside ourselves.

### Clip 1: Babette's Feast                    3 min.
*The General's speech.*

### Discuss                                        12–18 min.
What do you think provoked the General's strange speech? Was it just pious phrases or was it from the heart? If the latter, then what had he realized?

What provoked the two old men at the end of the clip to abandon their differences and laugh over them?

We've been talking about our choices and the differences they make. But here the General says the opposite: "Our choice is of no importance." What do you think he means by this? Could he be right and, if so, in what way?

"We even get back what we threw away." Does this imply that making a wrong choice doesn't matter?

What does the General mean by this? Is it the wine talking, or is he right?

Reader 1: Book of Numbers 13:1–2,
21, 23, 26–28, 30–33          *2 min.*
This story comes relatively soon after Moses led the Israelites out of Egypt and into the desert. Because of the choice they made here, they spent a further forty years as desert nomads:

> The Lord said to Moses, "Send men to spy out the land of Canaan, which I am giving to the Israelites...." So they went up and spied out the land.... And they came to the Wadi Eshcol, and cut down from there a branch with a single cluster of grapes, and they carried it on a pole between the two of them. They also brought some pomegranates and figs....
>
> And they came back to Moses and Aaron and to all the congregation of the Israelites in the wilderness of Paran, at Kadesh; they brought back word to them and to all the congregation, and showed them the fruit of the land. And they told him, "We came to the land to which you sent us; it flows with milk and honey, and this is its fruit. Yet the people who live in this land are strong, and the towns are fortified and very large...."
>
> But Caleb quieted the people before Moses, and said, "Let us go up at once and occupy it, for we are well able to overcome it." Then the men who had gone up with him said, "We are not able

to go up against these people, for they are stronger than we.... All the people that we saw in it are of great size...to ourselves we seemed like grasshoppers, *and so we seemed to them.*"

*Discuss*                                         *5–10 min.*

In this passage, what factor was overlooked by those who did not want to enter the land?

The old believers in the film knew their Bible. But did they really understand its significance? Grapes triggered a memory of this passage, but what might the story have taught them if they had understood it more fully?

*Clip 2: Shawshank Redemption*                  *9 min.*
*Red discovers hope on the outside.*

*Discuss*                                         *3–5 min.*
Does this clip remind you of the Gospels in any way?

Reader 2: Matthew 13:44

"The kingdom of heaven is like treasure hidden in a field, which someone found and hid; then in his joy he goes and sells all that he has and buys that field."

*Discuss*                                         *5–10 min.*
What do you understand by the kingdom of heaven and why does Jesus describe it as something so precious?

Is hope a feeling or a decision? Is it possible to behave hopefully, even if you do not feel it?

Reader 2                                             *1 min.*
The reading from Nelson Mandela in last week's meditation stated:

> Our deepest fear is not that we are inadequate.
>> Our deepest fear is that we are powerful beyond measure.
>> It is our light, not our darkness that frightens us.
>> We ask ourselves:
>> Who am I to be brilliant, gorgeous, talented, and fabulous?
>> Actually who are you not to be?
>> You are a child of God...[8]

*Discuss*                                            *5–10 min.*
Do you think this is true, that we fear our power more than our inadequacy? If so, why might this be?

*Ponder and Share/Brainstorm*                       *10–15 min.*
"Get busy living or get busy dying." Take some time to think about ways in which you might choose to "get busy living" to a fuller extent than before. Are there any choices which this course has offered for you personally? Think for a while and then share as you feel able. Write them down as a record of the choices you are making.
     and/or

What has been for you the most important lesson this course has taught you?

*Meditation*                                     *5–7 min.*

*Silence*                              *30 sec.–1 min.*

Reader 3:
Listen again to the old General's speech. Don't try to analyze it, but simply to absorb with gratitude God's gift to you of mercy and grace.

> Mercy and truth are met together, righteousness and peace have kissed each other.
>
> Man, in his weakness and shortsightedness, believes he must make choices in this life.
>
> He trembles at the risk he must take. We know that fear.
>
> But, no! Our choice is of no importance.
>
> There comes a time when our eyes are opened and we come to realize at last that mercy is infinite.
>
> We need only await it with confidence and receive it with gratitude.
>
> Mercy requires no conditions.
>
> And see, everything we have chosen has been granted to us, and everything we renounced has also been granted—yes, we even get back what we threw away.
>
> For mercy and truth are met together, righteousness and peace have kissed each other.

*Silence*                                          *30 sec.*

Reader 4: Romans 8:28

> We know that all things work together for the good of those who love God, who are called according to his purpose.

*Silence (or music)*                               *1–2 min.*

Use the time to think again over anything God might be saying to you through this course.

Reader 5: Prayer

> Lord, you want to give us a good land in which to dwell,
> yet very often we lurk around its desert edges afraid to enter in.
> Sometimes we feel like grasshoppers among giants,
> and to our shame, sometimes we would rather feel that way—
> because it absolves us from risk and from responsibility.
> Lord, help us to see where our small choices can make a difference in our world.
> And help us to see that we are not alone in making them:
> that at our weakest you come to us with hope,
> that you are with us in our journeying.
> And whether we get it right or wrong, you wait to enfold us in your grace.

For your mercy is infinite.
Thank you that you offer us redemption.
Thank you that you offer us to feast at your table.
We are grateful.
Amen.

*Silence*                                                      *30 sec.*

Reader 6/Leader
At the end of *Babette's Feast* the old believers, still full of the experience of grace the meal has given them, do a stately dance in the snow under the starlight. Let this, their song, be our benediction as we end this Lent course:

> The clock strikes and time goes by
> Eternity is nigh
> So let's use the remaining time to try
> To serve the Lord with heart and mind
> So that our true home we will find.
>
> Or, as Andy Dufresne would have said: "Get busy living or get busy dying."

*Silence*                                              *30 sec.–1 min.*

# THE HUMAN SCALE
## REDEEMED AND READY FOR ACTION

### Discouragement and Disappointment

Before writing the final session of this course, when I wanted to explore the General's strange speech about mercy, I looked back at the beginning of the film to remind myself where he was coming from.

The young Lorenz Lowenhielm clearly had very mixed motives in attending the group's religious meetings. His basic aim was to get the girl. But there was something else at work too. He had had "a mighty vision of a higher and purer life, free of debt and his father's censure, with a gentle angel at his side." What mattered most, to get his father and his financial burdens off his back, or to live a better life? His motives are unclear in the film, as are so many in real life.

But the group, and especially the girl's father, treated him with suspicion, and so he left, thwarted because he was unable to find either a welcome or a "way in" to the faith which half attracted and half repelled him. His conclusion as he departed was that "I have learned here that life is hard and cruel and that in this world there are things that are impossible."

It left me wondering how many other Lorenz Lowenhielms leave our Christian gatherings disappointed. How many have departed from my church feeling that it is impossible to belong there? How many have felt they were not accepted for who they were? How many felt the freeze of disapproval and discouragement because of mixed motives, wavering beliefs, or alien lifestyles?

## Confidence and "Can-Do"

When in the "guinea-pig" group for this course, we came to the question in the final session about fearing our power more than our inadequacy, one young woman in our group said she didn't fear either. Perhaps it was just her nature, she said. Perhaps she just took after her father who was renowned for his "can-do" attitude. She told us how, when she was little, her dad would take her on his knee and tell her how special she was. "If Margaret Thatcher can be prime minister of Great Britain," he told her, "then why shouldn't you do whatever you choose to do?"

Whether her father passed on a genetic gift of confidence, I couldn't say, but he certainly bestowed it by his words and actions.

In many of the previous examples I've given of people whose choices made a difference, there has been, hovering in the background, someone whose hidden role was simply to encourage. The parish priest, Trevor Huddleston, visiting a bright young teenager in a TB sanatorium and stimulating his mind with books and conversation. The teacher, Alice L. White, encouraging her pupils that, even though they were poor, black, and female, they should not set their sights lower than anyone else. The Vietnam War veteran returning in penitence to the place he once bombed and helping the peasants to take their economics into their own hands. The East London clerics crossing religious barriers and backing a humble night-shift cleaner to speak up for fair pay.

In William Wilberforce's case, it was a woman called Margaret Middleton.[9] She knew it was not in her power to campaign publicly about the evils of slavery or to bring about legislative change. But what she could do was act as a hostess to bring those who had influence together with those with a story to tell. She could not go to Parliament herself, but she could and did suggest to Wilberforce that he might be the man to do so.

And so Wilberforce, Rosa Parks, Desmond Tutu, Abdul Durrant in the East End, a handful of Laotian villagers, and a Kenyan pastor set out to change their world, secure in the confidence that someone somewhere believed in them.

## Solidarity and Support

One of the questions in Week Four was, *"If you were to write a letter a week about something you really cared about, what would it be?"* Our group came up with varied answers: the plight of political prisoners, violence on TV, world peace, trade justice, etc. Somebody wanted to wage a campaign on the proper use of the apostrophe! One person, a nursery teacher, said she wished she could write to parents suggesting they encourage their children more. As my thoughts spun off, I found myself wondering just how the world might be changed if each of us sent a message a week—a passing remark, phone call, email, text, letter, even a small gift—simply to let someone know that they were appreciated.

At the end of the last session, I suggested that you might share with others any choices you have decided to make. If you or anyone else did so, then well done! It was a brave step to entrust others with knowledge of your delicate half-formed plans. I want to suggest that the greatest gift you can now give one another as this course comes to an end is not to forget what was said. To keep it in confidence, naturally, but also to remind and reinspire one another, to show them you believe their choices, small or large, are both possible and positive.

If the only small choice this course provoked was that its participants began to encourage one another more, then I would be well pleased with my labors.

## Unexpected and Unconditional

I didn't set out to write a Lent course about the Easter story.

I wanted to write about what *we* could do. About how *we* can make good choices, about how *we* can make a difference, about the fact that inside our skulls is the most complex and powerful piece of matter in the whole universe, about how our tiny actions have the potential to affect big changes.

But again and again, as I have explored these themes, particularly in the films, I have been brought back to the idea that it's fear that so often prevents us from fulfilling our potential. That didn't surprise me—it's what any psychologist would tell you. What I didn't expect was that I would be brought back so inescapably to the place of the cross.

Not all of us are lucky enough to have had parents or teachers who believed in us. Many of us have had discouraging experiences of church. Some of us feel we have wasted years or, even worse, created irreparable damage to ourselves or others by making a wrong choice.

And I am left with the conclusion that for all of us there are times when there is simply nowhere else to go. Like Red at the end of *The Shawshank Redemption,* there are times when we no longer have the strength to lift ourselves up by our own bootstraps. Hope has run out. And so, in the final sequence, the film gives a new twist to its title. Andy provides for Red in the same way that Christ provides for us. It is called redemption—paying the cost for someone else to be set free, a generous unearned gift from a true friend. And that is the story of the cross.

In *Babette's Feast* too, the unexpected twist is redemption. For that surely is what the General—a vain, self-important man who lived his whole life to better himself and found it a hollow triumph—experiences at the feast. He has mouthed words about mercy before; now he feels it.

Why now? It is easy to understand how Babette's generous gift—of which only he understands the true cost—inspires both appreciation and awe. It is not surprising that meeting again the woman who once so moved him, stirs up longings that have lain buried for decades. But *"infinite mercy"*—where did that come from?

Perhaps from the same origins as Job's great and completely unexpected affirmation out of the midst of suffering: "I know that my Redeemer lives...!" (Job 19:25). Maybe from the same place as the light that struck down the Apostle Paul on the Damascus road, as the voice of a child that convinced Augustine while sitting in a Milan Garden, as the awareness of goodness that came to Dostoyevsky in a labor camp in Siberia, and to countless others, men, women, and children, who suddenly—out of the blue, it often seems—find themselves encountering the divine. It comes to those who give God no name and those who know him by names quite alien to us. For who are we to dictate to whom God should give his grace?

That is what redemption is all about—the undeserved, the unexpected, the unconditional. It is about a gift given by God—the amazing gift of grace.

## Important *and* Unimportant

The writings of the Apostle Paul sometimes confuse and occasionally infuriate me. But because Paul himself had such a powerful and unexpected experience of grace, there are times when he gets to the heart of the matter with breathtaking clarity. I think the following statement, like the speech the old General, must have come from one of those moments: "For by grace you have been saved through faith, and this is not your own doing; it is the gift of God—not the result of works, so that no one may boast..." (Eph 2:8–9). This passage is breathtaking not just in its clarity but in its paradox. First it states unequivocally that there is nothing whatsoever we can do to earn a state of grace. That can only ever come to us as a gift, taken on trust.

But then Paul goes on to turn it right around: "For we are what he has made us, created in Christ Jesus for good works, which God prepared beforehand to be our way of life" (Eph 2:10). In that they can never *earn* us the grace of God, our choices are of *no* importance. But in that God created each one of us unique, with contributions to the life of the world that only we can make, then that makes our choices of the *greatest* importance.

And here lies the deepest paradox: that only by accepting the grace—and the *un*importance of your choices—are you fully set free to make the sort of wise, selfless, and brave choices that could well be of the utmost importance in making the world a better place to live in.

### Forward Not Backward

When I test-ran this course, several members of the group suggested new sources of ideas and quotes. One was the Ray Bradbury story I quoted in Big Picture 5. Another was a film: *Pay It Forward*.[10] The plot revolves around a teacher (Kevin Spacey) who gives his pupils an unusual social studies assignment. They are to "Think of an idea to change the world and put it into action." Many of the kids complain at what they see as "weird," "too hard," "crazy," "a bummer." But twelve-year-old Trevor (Joel Hayley Osment) thinks up a plan. He decides that if he performs three big acts of generosity and then asks the recipients to "pay it forward"—do the same for three others—then good deeds should soon begin to multiply at an amazing rate.

At first everything he tries seems to turn to disaster. But then a journalist from a far-away state comes to visit. He explains that he is tracking down a story that began when his car was smashed and a complete stranger gave him a brand new Jaguar. The stranger's only explanation was that he was "paying it forward," and the mystified journalist decided to find out what was going on. The story ends tragically, but not before Trevor realizes that paying it forward does work after all.

It is paying it forward that is at the heart of everything Jesus lived and died for. He was trying to show us that when we truly understand the enormity of God's gift of grace and mercy, we realize it is a gift we can never pay back. We can only *pay it forward*—maybe not in huge dramatic acts, but certainly in a lifetime of small ones. Each tiny choice for the good is a "thank you" for the greatest good of all.

Most of you reading this will be familiar with the Easter story. Some may not. Either way, I hope you may see it, and its impact on your life, with fresh eyes this Eastertide.

—

"You received without payment; give without payment" (Mt 10:8).

## Small Experiment of the Week

If you have experienced God's grace and redemption in your life, then perhaps you could pay it forward by sharing with someone else that it might be possible for them too. A few simple words will do. "What are you doing over Easter?" might be the only cue you need.

# CONCLUSION

*Anyone can count the number of seeds in an apple,*
*but only God can count the number of apples in a seed.*

— Robert H. Schuller

*Change comes from small initiatives which work,*
*initiatives which imitated become the fashion.*
*We cannot wait for great visions from great people*
*for they are in short supply at the end of history.*
*It is up to us to light our own small fires in*
*the darkness.*

— Charles Handy

# HOW SMALL CHOICES
# MAKE BIG CHANGES

Have you ever played the "six-degrees of separation" game?

The theory is that everyone on our planet is connected to everyone else by a chain of only six people. In a recent experiment where 60,000 people were each assigned a "random target" to reach by email—a Norwegian vet, for example, or an Australian police officer—it took on average between five and seven emails to reach the target.[1] And it doesn't just depend on email. Choose any two people out of the world's six billion and you can construct a relatively short chain of personal acquaintance between them. Try it. Chances are that a London plumber or Welsh teacher really does know someone who knows someone who knows someone who knows someone who knows someone who knows a Polynesian fisherman.

## A Train of Events

The implications of this connectedness are mind-blowing. Your life might even now be affecting others in ways you could never have dreamed of.

This idea came home to me a little while ago when we were visited by a couple of long-lost friends from Seattle. The wife, Wendy, had stayed in our home some twenty-five years previously and, although we kept in contact for some years afterward, eventually we lost touch. But in a recent visit to London, they looked us up. We were surprised and pleased when Wendy told us how much our hospitality all those years previously had meant to her. "I decided that when I had a home of my own I wanted it to be like that," she said, "to be as welcoming to others as you were to me." She showed us photos: laughing groups on a sunny porch, barbecues overlooking a bay, their children in the arms of honorary aunties, and we could see that many of those smiling faces were Koreans, newcomers who had crossed the Pacific in search of work or education.

And suddenly into my mind came a picture. It was of a little ripple of hospitality spreading around the globe: from our little terrace house in South London to a ranch-style home on a hill—from there to an apartment in Seoul, on to a house in Ho Chi Minh city, a hill town in Thailand, a peasant hut in Burma. Maybe it's even now making its way across the Mongolian steppes!

I'm being fanciful, of course. But who knows? Certainly, Wendy and Michael's warm, welcoming home far outstripped ours. Who can say whether that little drop in the pond became a ripple that might even yet go on to become a wave?

And what about the youth group I helped run in the 1970s? We had a reunion last year, twenty-five years on (how scary is that!), and discovered that a surprising number of them are still committed to following Christ. One of them is a vicar. At least two of their offspring are currently doing relief work in the

Third World. I'm not claiming any great credit there—there were far better influences on them than me—but who knows which among their children's children may yet turn out to be the Mother Teresa, the Wilberforce, the Mandela of their generation?

## A Means of Growth

When people ask what I'm up to and I tell them I'm writing a book, they're often impressed. "How do you do it?" they ask. "I could never embark on something that big," they say. It's very gratifying—although perhaps when they see this volume they'll realize it's not exactly *War and Peace!*

I'm similarly impressed with the people I know who run marathons, cycle across the Sahara, build their own homes, translate the Bible into obscure languages, become bishops or leading experts on biodiversity. But just as I know that my first steps into writing involved enrolling for an evening class and writing articles for the church magazine, I also know that the bishop started out helping to run the youth group, and the biodiversity professor started out needing extra tutoring for less-than-good grades. The marathon runner started with a jog around the block and the cyclist started with a ride to the next town. I'm not sure about the Bible translator or the home builder, but I'd take a bet that theirs were similarly humble beginnings. Because, of course, that is the only way to start. Anyone who sets off to run a marathon or write a book without previously testing their abilities and learning the right skills is doomed to failure.

You don't become an expert on biodiversity by learning everything about every species in the world. Apparently—and I only know this because said expert lived with us for a while—it has more to do with finding out in mind-numbing practical detail which bugs inhabit which holly bushes and which beetles live in a certain patch of rain forest.

And you don't become a bishop just on theological erudition and an extremely holy demeanor. You first have to have been a seminarian getting your summer pastoral experience while photocopying newsletters and unblocking the church drains and learning how to handle all the demanding/obstreperous/recalcitrant/flaky/eccentric characters who seem so attracted to church life.

And so, by the time you embark on the big task you are not daunted because by now you know that it is only made up of lots of small tasks minute after minute, hour after hour, day after day. It happens one step at a time, one word after another, one brick upon the next.

## A Link in a Chain

I like bananas and I'm quite prepared to eat plenty of them. But however hard I try, my consumption of fair-trade bananas will not bring economic justice to the world. Even my friends George and Margaret's faithful selling of Traidcraft and Tearcraft will not do so. But if

I and George and Margaret and all the members of our parish church, and all the members of a hundred, a thousand other churches do so, and together we persuade a million friends and neighbors, a few supermarkets, a bank here and there, a handful of Congressmen and women, then en masse we really can do it. Bananas and coffee today, rice and tomatoes tomorrow, then maybe trainers and televisions and milk and medicines the day after. One day, just as the Berlin Wall fell and Communism crumbled with it, so globalization and greed and a world built on purely economic values will suddenly become just as untenable. I hope I live to see it!

## A Light in a Dark Place

> For many people the heavy responsibilities of home and family and earning absorb all their time and strength. Yet such a home—where love is—may be a light shining in a dark place, a silent witness to the reality and love of God.[2]

You may feel you can do very little to make the world a better place. The demands of a job, young children, or dependent relatives take all of your time and energy right now. Be comforted. Remember, firstly, that God does not demand the impossible. Take as your motto this verse from the Prophet Micah: "[A]nd what does the LORD require of you but to do justice, and to love kindness, and to walk humbly with your God?" (Mic 6:8).

Remember, secondly, that even if you are not making things dramatically better, you are undoubtedly preventing them from becoming worse.

If you are working hard and honestly, supporting your family and paying your taxes, bringing up a future generation who are educated and emotionally stable, treating your neighbors with courtesy, then what you are doing is great indeed. Your little home and your little workstation are not only lights in the darkness, but also bulwarks against a flood of negativity and disorder that might otherwise drown out peace and goodness.

One of my favorite quotes is from the very end of George Eliot's classic novel *Middlemarch*. She is speaking of her heroine Dorothea, who as a young woman so wanted to do something noble and splendid, but in the end becomes, like most women of her time, simply a wife and mother:

> Her full nature...spent itself in channels that had no great name on the earth. But the effect of her being on those around her was incalculably diffusive: for the growing good of the world is partly dependent on unhistoric acts; and that things are not so ill with you and me as they might have been, is half owing to the number who lived a hidden life and rest in unvisited tombs.[3]

## A Comfort in Failure

*In order to do something well, you first have to consent to do it badly.*

I don't know where that saying came from, but I know that when I first heard it, glaringly obvious though it is, it struck me with startling force and clarity. The following saying is my variation on the theme and, again, it is glaringly obvious but rarely considered: *In order to succeed, you first have to be willing to fail.* Again and again as I have explored the idea of choice, the words "fear" and "risk" have come up as inevitable companions. I know how often I have flunked demanding choices for fear of falling flat on my face.

In fact, as we go through life, failure is not just a risk but, at some time or another, a certainty, because none of us, bar one, is perfect. All of us get things wrong. All of us make choices that turn pear-shaped at some time or another.

And we cannot predict the consequences. The moment of inattention on the highway may result in a lucky escape, a scraped side mirror, or a pile-up. The unplanned pregnancy may result in a happy marriage, years of conflicts and compromises, or a hard lonely road of single parenthood. It may bring hidden regrets or unexpected delights—and probably both.

And it is because such failure and pain are intrinsically part of life that the redemption of the Christian Gospel is such a marvelous and, indeed, necessary gift. You'd think it would be glaringly obvious, but how often we fail to seek it out, or to respond when it unexpectedly seeks out *us*.

Redemption is not just for big mistakes and big disasters. It is there for small ones too. It is part of the daily experience of living in relationship with an interactive and redemptive God. It is not just about forgiveness, although that is part of it. It is also about restoration, about new beginnings. We have a God who not only works with us to bring added value to our positive choices, but also to bring good outcomes when things go wrong.

Easter is a time of hope and new beginnings. I hope it may be so for you.

—

If you wanted to divert a mighty river into a different course and all you had was a single pebble, you could do it as long as you put the pebble in the right place to send the first trickle of water that way instead of this.[4]

I have set before you life and death, blessings and curses. Choose life so that you and your descendants may live, loving the LORD your God, obeying him, and holding fast to him; for that means life to you and length of days... (Deut 30:19–20).

# TO SUM IT ALL UP

## How Small Choices Make Big Changes

- Small choices influence others and can multiply exponentially.
- Small choices influence others who may in turn become big influencers.
- Small choices now prepare us for big choices later.
- A succession of small choices eventually achieves a goal.
- A lot of individuals making small choices can have huge cumulative effects.
- Failing to take action in small matters can allow evil to triumph.
- Small moments of inattention can have catastrophic effects.
- Small choices of faithful goodness can hold back evil.
- The choice to open yourself to Christ's redemption can bring a new beginning.

## What Is Needed for Good Choices to Flourish?

*Observation*

- Full awareness of the world around you moment by moment;

- The capacity to seize chance opportunities as they present themselves.

*Limitation*

- Acceptance of the constraints imposed by circumstance and the needs of others;
- Willingness to live within God's moral boundaries and the calling he has given you.

*Imagination*

- A capacity to look beyond the obvious and the freedom to take a risk;
- The creativity to envisage something new and use what you have available to bring it into being.

*Determination*

- The perseverance to keep going onward toward a goal;
- The realization that huge achievements are made by a series of tiny steps.

*Affirmation*

- The freedom from fear and the past that only God's grace can truly give;
- The encouragement of others who believe in you and allow you space to grow.

## What Science Shows Us

We live in a universe that incorporates within itself:

- *Change*—progress and variety come from an

accumulation of tiny changes leading to creatures of great beauty and intelligence.

- *Chance*—our world is full of a randomness that
  means life is not as fixed as was once supposed
  and is therefore full of latent possibilities.
- *Complexity*—everything is interconnected, tiny
  variations can make huge global changes.
- *Consciousness*—as far as we know, in the universe
  humans alone have a remarkable capacity for
  awareness, understanding, imagination, and creativity.

If this is the way God made the world, then it makes
sense that all these tiny choices we make could be far
more important than we think.

## Five Things That Are Enemies to Choice and Ways to Approach Them

*1. Faulty theology*

- Don't be so heavenly minded that you are of no
  earthly use.
- It's not all up to God and it's not all up to you—
  work in partnership.

*2. A repressive community*

- If you come across anyone who wants to make
  your decisions for you—don't let them.
- Beware those who use words to shame you and
  make you feel small.

### 3. Refusal to detach from the past

- Whatever went wrong in the past, don't allow it to hold you back now.
- Let your background be a springboard and not a straitjacket.

### 4. Fear of your own weakness

- Mistakes are the best way to learn—take the risk.
- God loves giant killers—act in the knowledge that he is with you.

### 5. Unwillingness to trust

- God works in mysterious, unexpected, seemingly random ways—go with the flow.
- God made you unique—expect that he may have some unique things for you to do.

## SETTING GOALS

Although this course is about small choices, it will inevitably have also brought up thoughts about long-term goals. I have found the following guidelines, adapted from an exercise program,[5] to be wise advice in several different circumstances:

- Goals must be believable.
- Goals must be clearly defined and understood.
- You must want your goals badly enough.
- Goals must be put down in writing.

- You should stipulate a date by which you hope to achieve each goal. These dates can be altered, but they give your goals a timetable.

- Keep looking back at your goal list. Constantly remind yourself of them. Check off those that have been achieved and keep reminding yourself of those achievements.

- Set yourself different goals for different timetables—next week, one month, three months, a year or three years' time.

- *Live for today.* Don't worry about tomorrow, but don't put off till tomorrow what you can do today.

- Start behaving like the person you want to be.

- Expect setbacks. Laugh at them and learn from them. Pick yourself up and move on.

## ADDED EXTRAS

*Man is free, for he is in the image of divine liberty; and that is why he has the power to choose.*

— Paul Evdokimov

*The power of choosing between good and evil is within the reach of all.*

— Origen

## FOR INDIVIDUALS OR GROUPS

# STUDY
## CONSCIOUS—BUT NOT SELF-CONSCIOUS

### A Study of Genesis 3

It seems that this story has been simmering under the surface of much that I have been exploring throughout this course. I kept resisting the urge to go more deeply into it, because I know how many complex issues it raises. In the end, however, I concluded it could not be ignored, and so decided to give it a chapter to itself as an optional extra.

My reluctance was not surprising as this is a passage fraught with problems—first and foremost the age-old argument about whether it speaks about real or mythical events.

"Myth" is a word that often raises believers' hackles—understandably since one of its meanings is of "a commonly held belief that is untrue, without foundation."[1] But this is a shame because it is its other meaning that really matters here: "an ancient traditional story...offering an explanation of some fact or phenomenon."[2] A myth is a story that sheds light on what it means to be human. It is a story that lasts down the generations precisely because it does express some truth about human experience that is beyond era or culture. Whether it originates in fact or fantasy is irrelevant to its purpose or effect.

Indeed, I sometimes wonder if those who are most insistent on the historical veracity of Adam and Eve are those who most miss the point, because it then becomes easy to dismiss the story as being about *"them—then,"* whereas it only really begins to apply its truths when seen as *"us—now."*

Even so, quite what truths it embodies is a matter of dispute and some confusion. Perhaps its problem (and its genius) is that, like all the best myths (the parables of Jesus are a prime example), it holds within it layer upon layer of ideas, leaving us free to find in it the meaning most appropriate for us at any given time.

So I am going to take from this story some of the things it has meant to me, in full knowledge that there are still many questions unanswered and a great deal more meaning still left unexplored.

## Before You Begin

Offer God your willingness to "brain-stretch" rather than "knee-jerk."

Read through the whole story: Genesis 2:8–3:24.

Try to identify your preconceptions and put them aside. Accept that this passage will mean different things to different people. Expect you are more likely to learn from the questions it raises than the answers it gives.

## For Discussion

What view of this story—history or legend—were you fed when you first heard it? Has your view changed? How do you see it now and why?

What preconceptions did you bring with you to this story? For example, what kind of fruit did you think it talked about? Did you think it was about one tree or two? What kind of change did you think eating the fruit brought about? Does the temptation have anything to do with sex?

## The Orthodox Version—According to Whom?

> Therefore, just as sin came into the world through one man, and death came through sin, and so death spread to all because all have sinned.... Yet death exercised domination from Adam to Moses, even over those whose sins were not like the transgression of Adam.... For just as by the one man's disobedience the many were made sinners, so by the one man's obedience the many will be made righteous (Rom 5:12, 14, 19).

The interpretation of this story that I was given when I first became a Christian was that it was about something called "original sin." It's not a term that derives from the story in its Old Testament form—it may come as a surprise to discover that the word "sin" doesn't actually appear—but from Augustine's later commentary on the Apostle Paul's interpretation of it in his Letter to the Romans as quoted above.

But actually I can see the point Paul is trying to make in that first passage. It *is* a story about disobedience. It is a story about sin in that Adam and Eve both chose an action that had bad outcomes. Although I personally find it hard to comprehend the implication that we are all suffering because of one slip-up on Adam's behalf, Paul makes it clear enough that sin is, indeed, a disease all humans share.

But I think that the point the Apostle is really trying to make here is not just about Adam but about Jesus. (And to give him further due, he is struggling to understand recent events that will change the course of religious perception!) He is trying to show how, if the tiny choice of one man could change the course of history, it should not seem impossible that the choices of another man, Jesus Christ, could alter the seemingly inevitable human pattern of shame, blame, and retribution. Paul's message is a vital one, but I sometimes wonder if down the centuries it may have obscured at least one of the intentions of the original Genesis story.

## For Discussion

Forget for the moment the idea of Adam and Eve as a historical story and think of it entirely as a picture of your own experience. What echoes, if any, do you find in your personal history?

## The Moment of the Discovery—of What?

"[F]or God knows that when you eat of it your eyes will be opened, and you will be like God, knowing good and evil." Then the eyes of both were opened, and they knew that they were naked..."I heard the

sound of you in the garden, and I was afraid, because
I was naked; and I hid myself" (Gen 3:5, 7, 10).

Were Adam and Eve automatons up to this point,
unable to discern right from wrong?

If so, it doesn't say much for the freedom of human
choice. But the previous verses have already spoken of
man and woman created "in the image of God." They
have spoken of God's command to "rule over every living creature," and of God's delegation to Adam of the
choice of language: "whatever he called each living
creature, that was its name." It seems they had already
been given a great deal of freedom and of choice.

So if they already had the capacity to evaluate and
decide, what was the meaning of the "knowledge of
good and evil" of which they ate?

To answer that question, I think we need to look
at the result of that impromptu picnic. It was not further rebellion, not liberation, not dignity, but *shame*.

Suddenly what was most natural, their nakedness,
became an embarrassment. Suddenly, rather than
increased freedom, came the painstaking and ridiculous
task of sewing fig leaves. Suddenly, rather than pleasant
evenings spent in conversation with God, they found
themselves hiding from him.

To me the story of Adam and Eve is not only a
story about sin, but also about shame. It is a story
about the perversion of *consciousness*—the gift that
makes the human brain the pinnacle of the whole of

creation—into warped *self-consciousness,* the curse that arrives for most of us at some point around adolescence and dogs our footsteps forever afterward. In that light, the "knowledge of good and evil" is not describing a head-knowledge—something they must have had the potential for in order to do the "ruling" to which God had already commissioned them. Rather, it was a gut experience of what it is like no longer to *feel* good. It is an experience of no longer being at one—with each other, with the creation, with the Creator. It is the experience of being on our own in an alien universe.

It can be likened to experience that gradually creeps over us, in fact, throughout puberty, when we write our journals and play our albums filled with existential angst, when we feel ashamed of our bodies, awkward with the opposite sex, alienated from our ignorant and outdated parents, and frequently dismissive of whatever worldview has been carefully taught us for the last decade and a half.

## For Discussion

Were your teenage years rebellious or cautious? Do you think it is possible to grow to a mature understanding of life without a period of rebellion?

## The Suppression of Freedom—Or Is It?

> Dust is only a name for what happens when matter understands itself.[3]

Dust—the physical evidence for original sin...the physical proof that something happened when innocence changed into experience....[4]

During the years of puberty, they [children] begin to attract Dust more strongly....[5]

Better a world with...no Dust than a world where every day we have to struggle under the hideous burden of sin.[6]

If it comes about that the child is tempted, as Eve was, then she is likely to fall.... And if this temptation does take place and the child gives in, then Dust and sin will triumph....[7]

I cannot claim this idea of the story as related to consciousness and puberty as entirely my own. It is one strongly put across by Philip Pullman in *His Dark Materials,* the trilogy of children's stories from which the quotes above are taken. Pullman uses the metaphor of Dust (not literal dust, but elementary particles of some kind that cannot normally be seem) for consciousness. His young heroine, Lyra, is described as the second Eve. In his imaginary world, the Church is bent on the destruction of Dust because it believes it to be the source of all the world's ills. And that means that it is also bent on the obliteration of choice and freedom.

I want to take a moment to explore these views, because they seem to be opinions not just about the Church but also about the significance of the Adam and

Eve story that many share. This anti-Church perspective claims that the Genesis story has been used not only to suppress independent thinking but also sexual liberty.

This perception is backed up by the ending of Pullman's story, when Lyra and Will move from childhood to adulthood and become lovers (exactly what that means is discreetly veiled), the erosion of Dust is halted, and Lyra has fulfilled her mission by falling to temptation and becoming the second Eve.

Wonderful as Pullman's story is, and as much as I believe in the power of human love, this seems to me a slightly flawed conclusion—and, in fact, within the story there are other much stronger explanations of how Will and Lyra effect a salvation both when they visit the world of the dead to free them and when they choose to sacrifice their love by separation in order to stop the flight of Dust. (I don't just mean that they are stronger because of their resonance with the Christian view. They also seem to make more sense both in terms of the plot and of the wider reality of human experience.)

But it seems to me that there is nothing in the Genesis story as it stands to promote the idea that sexuality is shameful per se or to be avoided. Although it is a story about shame and the awareness of sexual difference, it seems to me that this comes only when the relationship with God is breached and not when it is whole. It comes as a consequence, not as a cause or as a punishment.

And the Genesis story is not saying that we cannot or should not think for ourselves. It is clearly a story that begins with a great deal of responsibility, "the LORD God put him in the Garden of Eden to work it and take care of it," and a great deal of freedom, "You are free to eat from any tree in the garden..."

Any tree except one, that is. It *is* a story about boundaries. It reminds us that life free from any restriction is impossible. It tells us that the down-side of consciousness and choice comes when curiosity takes over and the one thing outside our reach becomes the one thing we most want to grasp.

### For Discussion

Do you see this story as a tool for the suppression of freedom? If so, in what way?

Of all the temptations to move beyond the boundaries of responsible human behavior, it is arguable that sexual temptation is the hardest to resist. Do you think that is so?

### The Blessing of Consciousness—or the Curse?

> A single human mind is of greater worth than the whole inanimate creation, for you and I can do to the creation what the creation, for all its awesome size, cannot do to us: we can observe it, measure it, explore it, and wonder at it. It is as if in us the universe becomes conscious of itself.[8]

This is a paraphrase of a quote from St. Augustine, who made it clear, quite early in the Christian experience, that as humans we were made for knowledge. We were made to explore and push the limits of our understanding. So to interpret the story of the Garden as a warning against the dangers of knowledge makes no sense at all. The universe itself would seem to have little purpose without anyone to be aware of it, and that awareness, it seems, can only come from us.

Not only were we made for knowledge, we were made with the capabilities to put that knowledge to practical effect and to understand the consequences of doing so. To relegate us to nothing more than blind obedience (which in practice usually means obedience to a self-elevated human authority) makes nonsense of the description of humanity that Genesis has already given. It means that we are made in God's image only in the sense that a plaster statue portrays a lion. We have fewer choices than a computer programmed to play chess.

But what the Garden story does tell us is that this supreme gift of choice has a flip-side, and that this is the price of being human. Theologian and physicist John Polkinghorne explains:

> [I]t is better for God to have allowed a world of freely choosing beings, with the possibility of their voluntary response to him and to each other, as well as the possibility of sinful selfishness, than to have created a world of blindly obedient automata.... It is a fundamental human intuition that we are better as we are, in all our flawedness, than we would be if we were

reduced to automatic action, however beneficially programmed that action might be.[9]

So this very dignity of free choice, which we value so much, must bring with it the possibility of things going terribly wrong. Management Consultant Charles Handy recognizes the inevitable link:

> As I grew older, I realized that what I was told was God's greatest gift to mankind—choice—was in itself a paradox, because it gave the freedom to choose wrongly, to sin. You cannot have one without the other. Original sin is the price we pay for our humanity.[10]

So here we are again in the territory of paradox.

And I think there is one more paradox, much less frequently explored, that we must take into account. It is that the wonderful gift of consciousness brings with it the inevitable curse of self-consciousness.

It is self-consciousness that causes us to compare ourselves with others. It was self-consciousness that brought Cain to murder, Hitler to seek world domination, and Imelda Marcos to buy shoes. It is self-consciousness that causes us not to try for fear that we will fail, to keep our head below the parapet for fear of embarrassment, to put other people down so that we will look better, to spend our money in creating the image we want others to see of us. It is self-consciousness that disconnects us—from each other, from the natural world, from God.

And here I am brought full circle to the Apostle Paul's explanation in Romans, an argument kicked off by a breathtaking assertion: "Jesus Christ, through whom we have now received reconciliation" (Rom 5:11). Paul asserts that Jesus came to effect a reconnectedness we could never manage by ourselves. It is an assertion backed up by the experience of millions of Christians down the ages, who have discovered that only in Christ are they able to shake off self-consciousness and shame and become more loving, more free, and more fully aware of the glories in the world around them.

This train of thought has also led me to ponder another familiar Bible passage—the one where Jesus explains that "those who lose their life for my sake will find it" (Mt 16:25) and that a would-be follower must "deny [him or herself] and take up [his or her] cross" (Mt 16:24). And I've been wondering whether this self-denial has something to say not just about physical hardship and giving up chocolate for Lent, but also about letting go of our precious sense of self-identity. Perhaps it is only when we let go of the restrictions our self-consciousness puts on us that we can truly follow in Christ's footsteps and enter into a much greater awareness of life in all its fullness.

## For Discussion

In what ways does self-consciousness restrict the choices you make?

Are there any ways in which shame and guilt hold you back from fulfilling a potential you know you hold?

> Work like you don't need the money
>> Love like you've never been hurt
>> Dance like nobody's watching
>> Sing like nobody's listening
>> Live like it's heaven on earth...[11]

## MEDITATION
### TALENTS—BUT NO CONTEST

### A Meditation on Matthew 25

Do you remember one of those trivial quiz shows that was on TV a decade or so ago? I've forgotten its name, but the essence was simple. The audience was shown a word, take "tea" for example. They then had to say which other words they most associated with it: "cup," "time," "bags," "leaves," and the contestants had to guess which association topped the list. I've no idea whether they ever did it for the word "talent," but, if they did, I would guess that "contest" topped the list. And therein perhaps lies one of our greatest problems with this passage.

This passage from Matthew 25 is another one that I have grappled with. I can't claim that my struggles are over. There are some hard questions raised by this story that still trouble me and I can't promise you easy answers. However, the process of grappling has taught me an immense lesson, and so I offer this outline in the hopes that it may spark in you some of the same awe and wonder it has provoked in me.

## Before You Begin

Offer God your willingness to engage with the real, complex Gospel of Jesus. Let go of any presuppositions you may carry.

Read through the whole story: Matthew 25:14–30. Remember that it is a *story*, not a doctrinal statement.

Note any parts that make you uncomfortable. Give your discomfort to God.

Settle yourself in expectancy—you are on a journey with God.

## What Gifts Have You Been Given?

> "[T]o one he gave five talents, to another two, to another one..." (Mt 25:15).

Remember the story of beginnings in Genesis. The eating of the fruit brought self-consciousness and self-consciousness led immediately to shame. The first mention of sin came not with the eating of the fruit, but as the legacy of this awareness: *comparison*. It was the inferiority that Cain felt in relation to his brother that led to anger and the first murder.

So leave aside for a moment any question of comparison between yourself and others. Forget "talents" in terms of anything you excel at, for that will lead you inevitably back to comparisons. Look for a while at the very ordinary things you have been given—the minutiae of astonishing gifts that make up your daily existence:

- Consider how your brain commands your fingers. You decide to turn a page, and without even consciously registering it, the thing is done.

- Consider the number of images your eyes are sending to your brain each second, how it stores them away in memory to be recalled when needed, how without even being aware of it, you interpret those images—the time of day from the quality of daylight, the mood of a person from the set of their shoulders....

- Consider how you are able to translate the little black marks on this page into images and abstract ideas, how you are able to go beyond that and relate them to other stored ideas and experiences and so produce new concepts.

- Consider how you are able to explain those concepts to others, how together you can pass ideas back and forth and, if you wish, translate them into concrete action.

- Consider how you could choose right now to get up and dance, to sing, to pick wild flowers, to make an omelet, to chat on the phone to a friend.

Let your mind ponder for a few minutes on just how many amazing tiny opportunities your life affords you every second.

## How Do You Compare?

"[E]ach according to his ability..." (Mt 25:15).

For a long time I felt angry that this story comes down so hard on the one-talent guy. In my heart I was echoing the complaint our kids so often used: *"It's not fair!"* But as time went by I began to hear more and more the echoing reply we so often gave them: *"Life's not fair."*

Jesus is supremely realistic. He understands that life isn't fair. (Not that we would want it so, because the only way to achieve absolute fairness would be to have every human born with exactly the same physical and mental attributes—clones, in fact, and to give them exactly the same upbringing, exactly the same experiences and so on.)

And I have come to realize that Jesus couched the story in those terms precisely because he understood that unfairness—and that for most of us, our perception is that we are that one-talent person. A few perhaps are supremely confident and carefree, but most of us look at ourselves in comparison to others and find ourselves wanting. (And, in fact, those who sometimes look the most confident on the outside are the ones struggling most painfully underneath.) So look for a moment now at the comparisons you draw in your life:

- Consider the areas of your life in which you are most prone to make comparisons. List what they are.

- Consider the things you refuse to do for fear of failing or looking stupid. Think of an occasion when you did fail or look idiotic. How much did it really matter? How much did others really look down on you and how much was purely in your own head?

- Consider those you envy because of their position or privileges. If you were given those things tomorrow, would you be ready to deal with the responsibilities that come with them? Are you so sure that you would really want them?

- Consider those people you find difficult because they make you feel inferior. Could it be their way of dealing with their own insecurity? How have your feelings affected your relationship with them?

If these trains of thought have raised any prickles of anger or resentment, give them over to God right away. Take a few moments to focus again on what you have been given before going on to the next section.

## What Gifts Can You Use?

"Master, you handed over to me..." (Mt 25:20).

Take some time now to think about the gifts that God has entrusted to you and how they could be offered back. Remember it is not just about what you *do,* but who you *are:*

- Consider the simple, small actions you have at your disposal to brighten someone else's day. Make a list of everything you can think of.

- Consider how your combination of abilities and experience makes you unique. Think of just one thing this puts you in a unique position to offer.

- Consider the gifts you have that *aren't* unique to you or particularly impressive in any way. Might you be devaluing just how special these "ordinary" gifts actually are?

- Consider how much you feel a sense of "entrustedness." If you don't feel this, why might that be? Has someone robbed you of it?

## How Does Your View of God Influence Your Choices?

"Master, I knew that you were a harsh man..." (Mt 25:24).

But his master replied, "You wicked and lazy slave..."
(Mt 25:26).

Is the Master in this story a picture of God? If so, is he really the hard Master that is suggested? Why would Jesus portray him in this way if it were not so?

The whole of the rest of the Bible—especially the New Testament, and especially the words and actions of Jesus—portray a God who is loving, compassionate, merciful, forgiving, accepting, ready to give second chances. If you want to look at one example, I suggest that you take a little time with the story commonly known as the Prodigal Son.[12]

As I say, I don't have easy answers. The best way of understanding it that I can come up with is that we are again looking at paradox of two apparently opposing views:

(1) For God to be God he has to be pure goodness and diametrically opposed to waste and destruction.

(2) For God to be God he has to be pure love and totally accepting of the creatures he himself has made.

So the best response I can suggest is that we need to hold both these views together in creative tension. To take only one and completely jettison the other is to have a skewed perspective.

Look now for a moment at your perspective of God:

- Consider whether your view of God is of a hard taskmaster. If so, where did you learn this view? Are there any human influences, particularly in your upbringing, that colored your perspective?

- Consider how this view of a hard God affects your behavior. Does it induce fear, resentment, refusal?

- Consider whether you view God as uncritical and all-tolerant. If so, what are the pitfalls of taking this view to a logical conclusion?

- Consider whether you ever use this image of an all-forgiving God as an excuse for lapses, for which in your heart of hearts you don't really forgive yourself.

There is only one way to find out whether God really is a hard taskmaster or a loving Father, and that is not to run away from him but to trust him. Remember that the servant was not blamed because he failed. He was blamed because he didn't try. And he didn't try because he didn't trust.

## Must There Always Be Consequences?

"As for this worthless slave, throw him into the outer darkness..." (Mt 25:30).

Does this story point to a judgment and the possibility of eternal punishment? To me this is one of the most difficult issues raised by this passage, and I don't want to explain it away with glib answers, especially when the two stories that encompass it in Matthew 25 seem equally harsh.

(However, I would propose that these passages can be interpreted in ways other than everlasting torment. The original Greek word translated as "eternal" in verse 46 apparently doesn't necessarily denote going on forever, but endless in the sense of final, something that stands forever. The word translated "punishment" equally has a sense of curtailment or ending. And although the "eternal fire" referred to in verse 41 might seem to suggest torment, it is worth remembering that it is the nature of fire to consume, to change the state of what enters it, not to keep it in that same painful state forever.)

But some things in these passages do seem unarguable, even if we would rather not think about them too much. I suggest that just for a short while you take your courage in hand and consider them now:

- Consider that your actions have consequences that you might one day have to face.

- Consider that there will come a point in your life when your choices and chances stop, and that you have no way of knowing when it will be.

- Consider that you will one day meet your Maker. If you have learned to trust him, then you will know it is not something to be feared.

- Consider that in the final story in this chapter the King's evaluation is based not on doctrinal correctness but on small choices of compassion.

## How Does the Math Work?

> "Well done, good and trustworthy slave; you have been trustworthy in a few things..." (Mt 25:21).

> "For to all those who have, more will be given, and they will have an abundance..." (Mt 25:29).

But the good news is...this is not a story told to frighten us, but to spur us into action. It is to remind us that fear might be a good servant, but it is a very bad master. It is to promise us that if we do gather our courage in just a few small things, it will lead to a multiplication of effort and reward, and indeed that the rewards are likely to be spectacular. I hope that this is a process you have already begun to discover for yourself—maybe you just need reminding. If not, then try it. I think you will be pleasantly surprised.

- Consider how God has used your small moments of willingness. In what ways have they had rewarding consequences for yourself?

- Consider whether taking on responsibility has proved a burden or a blessing. If it has been a burden, why was that? Were you taking something on for the wrong reasons? Did others take advantage? If it accumulated blessings, what were they?

- Consider a time when you took a risk. Even if the act itself failed in some ways, what has the experience given you?

- Consider whether, in your experience, faithfulness in a few things has led on to bigger things. Has it ever worked for you the other way? Has a refusal of commitment in small things ever resulted in a lack of opportunities in larger things?

It's a risky business, this using of our talents. But how tragic if they remain forever buried, because we were scared to take the risk.

To laugh is to risk appearing the fool.
To weep is to risk appearing sentimental.
To reach out for another is to risk involvement.
To expose feelings is to risk exposing your true self.
To place your ideas, your dreams before a crowd is to risk their loss.
To love is to risk not being loved in return.
To live is to risk dying.
To hope is to risk despair.
To try is to risk failure.
But risks must be taken because the greatest hazard in life is to risk nothing.
The person who risks nothing, does nothing, has nothing, is nothing.
They may avoid suffering and sorrow, but they cannot learn, feel, change, grow, love, live.
Chained by their attitude they are slaves and forfeit freedom.
Only a person who risks is truly free.[13]

# FINAL EVENT
## A FEAST OF GIFTS

You may find you want to wrap up your Lent course with a special post-Easter celebration. If so, here is my suggestion: a Feast of Gifts.

I don't just mean a lavish meal, although, having watched *Babette's Feast*, that seems highly appropriate. Rather I mean an event where, in keeping with the course's broader theme, everyone comes with a small gift for others in the group.

And I don't just mean a sort of "Secret Santa"— gift-wrapped fripperies: socks or bath lotion. Rather I mean that each person think creatively of a way in which they might bless the others and enrich their lives:

- If you are musical, it might be bringing a song or a tune to play.
- If you are good at craftwork, you might make an individualized bookmark for each person as a memento of the course.
- If you enjoy literature or writing, you might bring a poem or a passage to share.
- It could, of course, be providing part of the meal.
- It might simply be to do all the clearing and washing up.
- It might be a comic song or a skit.

- It might be a sincere and carefully thought-out note of appreciation to each person for what they have brought to the group.

- It might be...oh, I don't know...it might be Mozart or some cold beers or a crate of books!

Be creative, pray about it, think laterally, spring a few surprises.

Whether you want to co-ordinate it or trust it all to happenstance, I leave to you. Certainly if food is involved, a degree of planning might be appropriate.

Whatever you come up with, here are a few ground rules:

- Don't spend a fortune. Leave that to Babette.

- Don't be too elaborate. You might want to give the food a French theme, but resist the urge to try *quaille au sarcophage* or turtle soup!

- Don't be afraid to take a risk. Risk has been a recurring theme in this course, and hopefully by now your group has become a secure environment within which to take a chance.

- Don't show off. This is about blessing others, not validating yourself.

- Do receive gratefully everything that is offered.

- Do make your appreciation and affirmation vocal and evident.

- Don't forget to give special thanks to the group

leader, if there has been one person doing the bulk of the work for the course as a whole.

Above all, take the opportunity for a few small choices you might not otherwise make. Don't take it too seriously. Have fun.

# LEADER'S NOTES

*Obedience demands of you*
*that you listen to the other person,*
*not only to what he is saying, but to what he is.*
*Then you will begin to live in such a way*
*that you neither crush nor dominate*
*nor entangle your brother,*
*but help him to be himself*
*and lead him to freedom.*

— Dutch monastic rule

# INTRODUCTION
## BEFORE YOU START

### Showing the Films

Ideally group members need to have seen both films before the sessions start, so try, if at all possible, to organize two pre-Lent introductory sessions in order to view the films.

You need to be aware, however, that there are copyright restrictions on public viewings of films. It is fine to show extracts as part of a course, and it is fine to show the whole film to course members, but what you cannot do is advertise the films as a public viewing, either free or with entrance fee. So make sure that your film showings are by invitation only, for people enrolled in the course.

If this is not possible, then make it clear to participants that they will get much more from the course if they have seen the films beforehand.

### Scheduling the Sessions

There are five group sessions to coincide with the five weeks of Lent (excluding the week of Ash Wednesday and Holy Week). At the end of the course (see Added Extras, pages 181–207) are two extra chapters on passages that are key to the subject, but would demand too much time if explored in full within the regular sessions (in fact, Matthew 25 comes in briefly in Week 3, and Genesis 3 in Week 4). The sessions are:

- "Conscious—But Not Self-Conscious": a study on Genesis 3.
- "Talents—But No Contest": a meditation on Matthew 25.

These can be used either for individuals or groups, so you might like to consider whether you want to run two extra sessions after Easter in order to include them.

## Celebrating the Course End

You might like to round off the course after Easter with a more light-hearted social event and the Feast of Gifts outlined on page 205 suggests a creative and interesting way of doing so.

## Timing Each Session

There are two timings beside each item in the group sessions. The total of the smaller numbers should give you a one-hour session and the larger numbers add up to an hour and a half.

Having said that, I have to admit that one of my main failings is trying to cram too much in, and you will find that there is a great deal of material here that could take a lot longer if you let it. In fact, to do it justice, expanding to two hours might be ideal.

It's up to you how you use the material so, of course, feel free to go off on tangents or take time with issues that have arisen from the individual reading, but if you do want to get through the material here, you will have to be pretty strict on sticking to the subject.

So discuss and decide with the group beforehand how long you want the sessions to be and exactly what the starting time is—and then stick to it!

## Using Video or DVD

Try as far as is possible to have clips set up and ready before you start. This is one example where old technology is better than new, because it is a lot easier to have a video ready at the right point, whereas with DVD, unless a clip happens to start at the beginning of a chapter, it can only be fast-forwarded through and left on "Pause" mode. This means if you are using both films on DVD, it takes more time to set up the second clip. Even if you have to fast-forward through at the time, try to do as much as possible off screen rather than on.

NB: remember to set the screen to the video setting so that you don't revert to a TV channel by mistake.

I have tried to give as accurate timings as possible, but these may vary from machine to machine. Do make sure you check the timings before you start, and especially make sure that, on video, the films are set to zero at the appropriate point:

- All video timings for *The Shawshank Redemption* come from setting the timer to zero at the point when Castle Rock Entertainment comes up as white text on black background, *after* Castle Rock logo with lighthouse.

- All video timings for *Babette's Feast* come from setting the timer to zero at the point when "Just Betzer presenterer" comes on screen above view of sea, *after* Metro Goldwyn Meyer logo of roaring lion.

## Knowing Your Material

I have tried to make this course as user-friendly as possible and so, where there are questions either about the films as a whole, or the broader biblical picture, I have given suggested answers in the notes for each session. However, there is no substitute for getting to know your material—both the films and the Scriptures—for yourself. I find that I need to have seen any movie at least twice in order to really come to grips with it, and so I would suggest the same for you. Try if at all possible to read through the session notes beforehand and think through your own answers—and questions—and explore what the Scripture passages have to say on the subject.

## Listening to the Group

I included the quote at the beginning of this section because good group leadership should always be more about listening than speaking. Here are a few suggestions for good listening:[1]

- Try to understand where group members are coming from. (For example, people may have a variety of church backgrounds and a wide range of expectations and understandings of what Lent is about.)

- If you are unsure what someone is trying to say, repeat back what you thought you heard, preferably using different words without changing the meaning. If in doubt, ask a question to try to tease out the background behind a particular comment.

- Notice the attitudes and feelings involved as well as a person's words. Be aware of body language and what it is saying.

- Listen for what people are *not* saying, as well as what is said.

- Resist the urge to respond with your own message, opinion, or advice. You are there to facilitate others, and chances are someone else in the group has something just as valuable to offer.

- If you sense that there is some deeper issue behind someone's words, then try to find out afterward if it is something that requires prayer or counseling. You need not be the one providing further help, but make it your business to help them seek it out if they wish it.

If you find that the group members are particularly incapable of listening to each other, then in desperation here are a couple of techniques:

- Have a small item—a shell, a pebble, a toy mouse!—and make a rule that only the person holding it can speak.

- Find some noise-making implement—bell, whistle—and agree to a maximum length for each contribution. Then appoint someone as time-keeper and noise-maker when the speaker's time is up!

# SESSION ONE
## THE CHOICE OF OBSERVATION

### Introducing Ourselves

It may be a good idea at this point to check on how many of the group members have managed to see both films through in full. (If arrangements are needed for lending videos or DVDs, etc., then do so at the end of session.) It might also be interesting to find out a bit about people's understanding of Lent.

Go over the group's ground rules (see page 33).

### Clip 1: *Babette's Feast*

**In:** DVD 14: 1 min. 10 sec. Video: 1 hr. 9 min. 58 sec.

As sherry is poured, just after General is seated at table and before "Remember we have lost our sense of taste."

**Out:** DVD 14: 3 min. 28 sec. Video: 1 hr. 12 min. 17 sec.

After "must be some kind of lemonade."

## Discuss: Readings

I chose these two readings to bring out the fact that, although Jesus told us that there were more important things than food, he also told us about a Father who loves to give us good things and, therefore, by implication, wants us to enjoy them.

## Brainstorm

List one: Shopping. Typical reasons for choice might be: time, bargains, fair-trade goods, organic, "buying American," choosing corner shop over supermarket, etc.

List two: Eating. Typical ways of eating might be having family meals together at table or in front of the TV, snacking on the run, entertaining, etc.

Try to extract from both these lists what they demonstrate about people's priorities.

## Clip 2: *Shawshank Redemption*

**In:** DVD 2: 2 min. 20 sec. Video: 13 min. 43 sec.

After Andy is hosed down and deloused, just as procession of new prisoners enters cage.

**Out:** DVD 3: 7 min. 50 sec. Video: 22 min. 10 sec.

After: "Doesn't matter what his name was.... He's dead"; just as it cuts to shower sequence.

## Discuss: Film Brutality

Be aware that violence is a very sensitive subject and that some people may have a painful history in that area. Make sure that no blame is apportioned, either to those who choose to watch violence or those who choose not to. (It might be worth pointing out that none of the extracts selected for future sessions are violent in any way.)

This discussion may also bring up issues of fiction versus fact on screen, as some people may say that they only watch news or documentary programs. It might be worth referring back to the introduction on the value of fiction as a means of understanding. It is also worth noting, of course, that whatever "factual" footage we see is highly selective. The boundaries between fact and fiction are increasingly blurred when it comes to the moving image, and the truth has to be sifted carefully from whatever we watch.

"What was his name?" This question is intended to draw out the idea that when we put a name to someone we can no longer ignore him or her. He or she becomes a real person to us and not just an idea. It might be worth going on to explore why the prisoners might choose to switch off from knowing too much.

# SESSION TWO
## THE CHOICE OF LIMITATION

### Opening                                    *1–2 min.*

Ground rules as before (see p. 33).

It is probably easier to deal with any really quick points from readings or previous sessions right away; schedule in anything else for later in session or for another occasion altogether if a major item arises.

### Clip 1: *Babette's Feast*

**In:** DVD 2: 00 min. 00 sec. Video: 1 min. 04 sec.

Just as last opening credit "Komposist—Per Norgard" disappears, before beginning of voiceover.

**Out**: DVD 2: 4 min. 40 sec. Video: 5 min. 52 sec.

After "great world outside," as soon as shot moves to flag and soldiers' parade ground.

### Discuss: The Sisters' Limited Lifestyle

Losses from different choices:

- loss of their father's approval;
- loss of the relationship with each other;
- loss of their faith, innocence, and devoutness;
- loss of confidence—out of their depth in sophisticated society.

Good things:

- they kept their faith;
- they held the little group of believers together;
- they did a great deal of good in their community;
- they were able to exercise leadership skills;
- they were able to help Babette;
- they had each other.

Perhaps it is worth pursuing what difference their faith made. Would they have accepted their limited life as serenely as they did without it?

## Brainstorm: Choices Which Limit Us

People may well point out that all the choices we make have benefits as well. It might be worth asking whether they think any choices have absolutely no personal gain (caring for a relative with Alzheimer's, for example, might come in this category).

"Becoming a Christian" may well be a suggested answer at this point, possibly bringing up the issue as to whether coming into faith is a choice that we make. Some people's experience may be that it was something they simply grew up with or that it was such a gradual transition that they never saw themselves as making a choice. Others may feel that God chose them, that their experience is of God confronting them, rather than them seeking God. Allow the freedom for people to express their own experience, without getting bogged down in an abstract "free will" versus "predestination" debate. However people come to faith, all present will probably agree that they could have chosen to walk away from Christianity and they have not.

## Discuss: Any Choice Without Limitation?

There will probably be a simple "no" answer to this question, which is why I didn't allow any time for it.

### Discuss: Narrowness

You may need to differentiate between the narrowness of the gate (the entry into faith) and the narrowness of the actual path (the Christian life). NB: Jesus refers to himself as both the gate (Jn 10:9) and, more famously, as the way (Jn 14:6).

The former may bring up questions as to whether Jesus is the only way to faith. For my money, the quickest answer is that yes he is in that his sacrifice was for all humankind, but no in that not all who come in may recognize this. A great fictional exposition of this is in chapter 15 of *The Last Battle* in C. S. Lewis' Narnia series, where one of the forces opposed to Aslan (the Christ figure) finds himself admitted to Aslan's country through the Stable door:

> The Glorious One [Aslan] bent down his golden head and touched my forehead with his tongue and said, Son, thou art welcome. But I said, Alas, Lord, I am no son of thine, but a servant of Tash. He answered, Child, all the service thou hast done to

Tash, I account as service done to me.... Therefore if any man swear by Tash and keep his oath for the oath's sake, it is by me that he has truly sworn, though he know it not, and it is I who reward him.... But I said...Yet I have been seeking Tash all my days. Beloved, said the Glorious One, unless thy desire had been for me thou wouldst not have sought so long and so truly. For all find what they truly seek.[2]

However, try not to focus on this aspect of the question, but the narrowness of actual Christian living.

My use of the word "destiny" is to provoke debate rather than because I actually believe in karma or fate. I do believe that each of us has a different and individual path—after all, we are all starting from different points, so it could hardly be otherwise. However, I would actively refute any idea of "miss it and you've blown it." God allows for freedom of choice, the inevitability of mistakes, and the possibility that we might miss the path through no fault of our own. I see God's plan for our lives as rather more like those in-car route planners that instantly recalculate and tell you the right direction from wherever you are at any given moment!

## Clip 2: *Shawshank Redemption*

**In:** DVD 2: 0 min. 00 sec. Video:11 min. 31 sec.

After Red makes bet with other prisoners, just before Andy walks under entry gate.

**Out**: DVD 2: 2 min. 46 sec. Video: 14 min. 16 sec.

After "Nothing left but all the time in the world to think about it."

### Discuss: Genesis 2

I know that any discussion of this passage is likely to demand far more time than I have given it here. The first problem is that it is likely to provoke a "fact or legend" debate, which raises difficult issues about the nature of Scripture itself. These are important issues but resist them now, as hard as you possibly can!

I have included an in-depth study of this passage in Added Extras "Conscious—But Not Self-Conscious," pages 182–194. If the group hasn't looked at it already, then refer them to it for further study.

I have included the passage here because, despite its difficulties (which means it is often somewhat sidelined these days), it is still a great story for provoking thought about the nature of obedience, choice, guilt, and the consequences of wrongdoing.

Some pointers from that study which might be worth reiterating:

- Rather than looking at this as a story about the first man and the first woman, it might yield more understanding when looked at as a story of Everyman and Everywoman.

- A new way of looking at it might be to substitute the phrase, "knowledge of good and evil," with an alternative: "the experience of good and evil." Since it deals so clearly with the experience of shame, this is not such an off-the-wall interpretation.

- Consider whether the command not to eat the fruit might have been a permanent prohibition or a temporary one (like banning a small child from playing with matches, or eating unripe fruit).

*What other choices could Adam and Eve have made?*
We tend to forget that it was not just a choice between blind obedience or disobedience on a whim. They could also have:

- waited for a while to see if the prohibition was lifted;
- discussed it with God (after all, he walked nightly in the garden with them);
- tried to persuade God to change his mind;
- used their logic to try to understand why the prohibition was in force;
- considered whether God's word or the snake's was more trustworthy;
- chosen to leave the garden;
- chopped the tree down!

# SESSION THREE
## THE CHOICE OF IMAGINATION

### Clip 1: *Shawshank Redemption*

**In:** DVD 9: 7 min. 25 sec. Video: 1 hr. 1 min. 51 sec.

Just after Brooks kicks stool away, on pan down to hanging figure.

**Out:** DVD 11: 1 min. 43 sec. Video: 1 hr. 9 min. 26 sec.

Just after "Like Brooks did?"

### Brainstorm: Choices Andy Made

- Chose to write a letter a week, then chose to write two a week.
- Chose to play the Mozart for himself, then for others; chose to continue in moment of outright defiance.
- Chose to get rock hammer and give himself an interest carving stone.
- Chose to hide hammer in Bible.
- Chose to try to chip hole and escape.
- Chose to keep quiet, to keep to himself for a while, to think and not to harden himself.
- Chose to seize opportunity of overhearing guard talk about finances.
- Chose to get beer for others rather than privilege for himself.

- Chose to go along with turning financial work into business.
- Chose to go along quietly with Warden Norton's dodgy finances, biding his time.
- Chose not to give up hope.

## Discuss: Parable of the Talents

This is potentially a huge subject, but try to keep to the questions if possible, and refer the group to the meditation in Added Extras "Talents—But No Contest" on page 194.

Try to get the group away from assumptions about the idea of "talent" in its contemporary meaning of a gift or aptitude. It might be worth exploring what gifts or blessings those who are least conventionally "gifted"—with a physical disability or learning difficulties, for instance—bring to those around them. If you conclude that even those with the least abilities have something to give, then the "have" in this context must be something else. I would contend that the only thing you need to "have" in order to be given more in this context is the willingness to use what you've already got.

## Clip 2: *Babette's Feast*

**In:** DVD 16: 0 min. 0 sec. Video: 1 hr. 33 min. 52 sec.

Just after old man says "Hallelujah" outside in the moonlight.

**Out**: DVD 16: 2 min. 55 sec. Video: 1 hr. 36 min. 41 sec.

As candle dies, just after "And how you will delight the angels."

## Brainstorm: Other Risky Acts in the Bible

New Testament:

- Jesus going into wilderness and fasting.
- Disciples giving up all and following.
- Jesus being so outspoken with religious leaders.
- Peter walking on water.
- Peter standing up on Day of Pentecost.
- Paul deciding to plead his case before Rome.

Old Testament:

- God creating such an extravagant natural world.
- God creating humans with free will.
- Noah believing God and building an ark.
- Abraham deciding to uproot his family and follow where God led.
- Moses taking Israelites into desert.
- David dancing before the Lord.
- Jeremiah buying a field.
- Daniel defying Nebuchadnezzar.

## Brainstorm: Creativity with a Cost Through History

- Galileo sticking to his scientific discoveries in the face of religious opposition.
- Building of Panama Canal.
- Settlers in the United States.
- Going into space.
- Michelangelo painting Sistine Chapel ceiling.
- Van Gogh continuing to paint, with only one piece of artwork sold during his lifetime.

Music: In view of the film clip, some Mozart might be a good choice. I used the first 2–3 minutes of the Clarinet Concerto, second movement.

# SESSION FOUR
## THE CHOICE OF DETERMINATION

### Clip 1: *Shawshank Redemption*

**In:** DVD 15: 15 min. 54 sec. Video: 1 hr. 47 min. 5 sec.

Just as Warden Norton enters cell, after he passes Red.

**Out:** DVD 16: 5 min. 22 sec. Video: 1 hr. 55 min. 5 sec.

At end of sequence where Andy stands in water with outstretched arms. (It might be a good idea to pause in order to freeze-frame the image on the screen for a few more seconds while people think about question 1.)

## Discuss

The final image in that clip is clearly evocative of many images of Christ, both on the cross and as an image of triumph: "It is finished." Others have also seen a reference to Baptism. As to whether it is deliberate, filmmaking is such an expensive and complex process that you can be sure that nothing is on screen by accident. The image was clearly intended to invoke the idea of redemption, although I don't think you can deduce from that any Christian motive on behalf of the director, or even that Andy was intended to be seen as a Christ figure.

Redemptions in the story:

- The central redemption was Andy's own, hard-won by his own efforts.

- Red also found final redemption as a result of Andy leaving the hidden money and sending the postcard.

- The setting-up of the library was redemptive in offering culture and education to inmates.

- The young boy who learned to read would have been redeemed by Andy's efforts, had the Warden not killed him.

- The exposing of corruption would have, with hope, led to the redemption of the prison system.

## Ponder and Share

Unlike most of these sections, where it has been better to give people the choice whether to participate or not, in this one it works well to go around the room and get everyone to state the thing they most care about changing.

## Brainstorm

It is probably true that there is virtually no advancement or benefit that *hasn't* come about by persistence, but let the group arrive at this conclusion by themselves.

## Ponder and Share

The reading from Luke could easily raise questions in people's minds about the problems of unanswered prayer, but that is probably best avoided as it is far too big a subject to go into at this point. However, be aware that it may be an issue for some people and, if so, try to find a way to deal with it at another time.

It might be worth questioning whether, even if the prayer is unanswered, the choice of persistence has positive spin-offs for the person doing the praying, or for the prayed-for situation in other ways.

## Clip 2: *Babette's Feast*

**In:** DVD 14: 6 min. 41 sec. Video: 1 hr. 15 min. 30 sec.

On wine being poured out, just after Babette says to the coachman, "This is good."

**Out**: DVD 14: 9 min. 26 sec. Video: 1 hr. 18 min. 14 sec.

Just after "Hallelujah."

## Discuss

Single-mindedness may quite rightly be seen by some as a negative attribute—it is true that single-minded people can often have a degree of ruthlessness that impacts on those around them, particularly family. Try to tease out the good and bad aspects of single-mindedness and what constraints, if any, it should have.

## Meditation: Mandela's Speech

People may well have found this powerful and want to talk about it more. Let them know that there will be a chance to revisit it next week.

# SESSION FIVE
## THE CHOICE OF AFFIRMATION

### Clip 1: *Babette's Feast*

**In:** DVD 14: 13 min. 51 sec. Video: 1 hr. 22 min. 40 sec.

As Eric brings fruit into the dining room, just after coachman tastes fruit in kitchen.

**Out:** DVD 14: 17 min. 11 sec. Video: 1 hr. 26 min. 40 sec.

Just after "Then I deserved it, dearest brother."

## Discuss: The General's Speech

Refer the group to where it is printed in full at the end of the session (p. 154).

It might be worth reminding the group of the circumstances of the choice which the General made as a young man.

As a young officer he has been leading a "merry life" and has fallen into debt. He is sent to his aunt's home on the coast of Jutland by his father to "think about your conduct and set about improving it." When he first sees the beautiful young Martine, he has "a mighty vision of a higher and purer life, with a gentle angel at his side." He begins to attend the pastor's meetings, but gradually begins to feel "more and more insignificant." His decision to leave comes at a meeting where the pastor speaks almost the exact words that he will repeat all those years later: "Mercy and peace are met together...righteousness and delight shall kiss each other...." (Note the subtle difference between "delight" in the first instance and "peace" in the second.) Bread is being passed around (the implication is that this is a communion, though that is unclear) and he chokes slightly on the bread.

It is evident that the pastor and his flock are watching the attraction between Martine and the young officer, and that the pastor, at least, wants to freeze him out.

So the young officer leaves, forever. "I have learned here that life is hard and cruel," he says, "and that in this world there are some things that are impossible."

He returns to his barracks and decides to forget the "pious melancholics who can't afford salt for their porridge" and give up on his love for the lovely Martine. "From now on," he declares, "I will think of nothing but my career and some day I shall be an important figure in the world."

His first step is to marry a lady-in-waiting to the Queen, and, since piety is fashionable in the court, to apply the pious phrases he learned at the parsonage to gain the Queen's favor. "We must implore God's mercy," he tells her as they waltz. "We must carry out the Lord's tasks with love."

**Reading** (Numbers 13:1–2, 21, 23, 26–8, 30–3)

(I have chosen to give the reading in this selected form because it is very long in full and crammed with difficult and distracting names!)

In the passage, the Israelites had failed to grasp the promise in verse 1 that God wanted to give them the land. The believers in the film had not understood that God might have wanted to give them, too, a life of milk and honey, but that fear had caused them not to take hold of it.

## Clip 2: *Shawshank Redemption*

**In:** DVD 16: 13 min. 52 sec. Video: 2 hr. 3 min. 35 sec.

Red packing at checkout, just after he is shown into room with sign "Brookes was here."

**Out:** DVD 18: 00 min. 00 sec. Video: 2 hr. 12 min. 5 sec.

Long shot of beach with Red and Andy meeting, just before "In memory of...."

It may be worth reminding the group that Andy had previously told Red that if he ever got out, he was to go to this place and find the wall and the stone that didn't fit. He had also told Red of the place in Mexico he would head to and had sent him a postcard to show he had arrived.

## Discuss: Does this clip remind you of the Gospels in any way?

What I had in mind initially was the image of the treasure in the field, but there are many other resonances as well. Some have said that it reminds them of the Prodigal Son, of the importance of friendship, of Christ's forgiveness. Perhaps the most important thing to bring out is that Andy can be seen as a Christ figure here, offering Red a redemption at the very time when his hope is gone and he is unable to lift himself out of his despair.

## Optional Extra Question

You might like to add the following question: How much is belief in the afterlife a spur to human achievement and how much is it a hindrance?

This question refers back to a quote from the film *Second Coming* near the beginning of the course (Big Picture 1, page 22) that "right now we're promised an afterlife, so we waste the seventy years we've got." However, it also raises a lot of issues to do with people's ideas about heaven, which could take up a lot of time and end up being something of a red herring, so use your discretion!

## Discuss: Why might we fear our power more than our inadequacy?

Answers might include:

- worry about where it might lead;
- the idea that power corrupts;
- fear of failure;
- the realization that power carries with it responsibilities.

In the groups which acted as guinea pigs, someone referred to Jesus' refusal to take on power in the temptations in the wilderness. It is worth realizing that Jesus did not refute the power he knew he had, but the temptation to use it in a wrong way.

## Ponder and Share/Brainstorm

People may choose to share quite major choices that are facing them. Especially in this case, but perhaps anyway, it might be good to offer prayer for those people who are facing choices. This could be done in the group as a whole, individually after the meeting, or perhaps left until the final night of the group feast.

**Reading:** Romans 8:28

I have chosen this verse in order to finish the course on an upbeat note, but clearly there are some people for whom life has been hard and painful, and for whom it might seem simplistic and over optimistic. Be aware of anyone in this situation and perhaps offer individual prayer or counsel at a later point.

# NOTES

## The Films

*Babette's Feast,* written and directed by Gabriel Axel from a short story by Isak Dinesen, starring Stephane Audran, Birgitte Federspiel, Bodil Kjer. Released by Panorama Film International 1987 and distributed by MGM Home Entertainment (Europe).

*The Shawshank Redemption,* written and directed by Frank Darabont, based on *Rita Hayworth and Shawshank Redemption* by Stephen King, starring Tim Robbins and Morgan Freeman. Released by Castle Rock Entertainment 1994 and licensed by Rank Film Distributors Ltd.

## Introduction

1. Mark Kermode, interviewed in *The 100 Greatest Films,* Tyne Tees Television.

2. *Casablanca,* directed by Michael Curtiz and released by Warner Brothers, 1942.

3. Richard Dawkins, *The Blind Watchmaker* (Harlow, Essex, England: Longman Scientific and Technical, 1986), p. 18.

4. Quoted by Keith Ward in *God, Chance and Necessity* (Oxford: Oneworld Publications, 1996), p. 44.

5. John Polkinghorne, *Science and Providence* (London: SPCK, 1989), p. 2.

6. John Steinbeck, *East of Eden* (Oxford: Heinemann, 1952), pp. 263–4.

## Week One

Opening quotations: Playwright Dennis Potter interviewed by Melvyn Bragg on Channel 4 just before his death in 1994; William Blake, poet and artist, *Jerusalem* (1815).

1. Russell T. Davies, *The Second Coming,* television drama.

2. Philip Pullman, *The Amber Spyglass* (New York: Scholastic, 2000), pp. 382 and 548.

3. David Boulton, "Face to Faith: The Republic of Children," *The Guardian,* April 5, 2003.

4. Philip Pullman interviewed by Melvyn Bragg on the *South Bank Show,* March 2003.

5. Philosopher of Religion David Pailin, quoted in Russell Stannard, *Science and Wonders: Conversations about Science and Belief* (London: Faber & Faber, 1996), based on BBC Radio 4 program, pp.132–3.

6. Pullman, *The Amber Spyglass,* p. 525.

7. Henri J. M. Nouwen, *Here and Now* (London: Darton, Longman & Todd, 1994), pp. 3–4.

8. Experiment conducted by John M. Daley and C. Daniel Bateson, in *Journal of Personality and Social Psychology,* Vol. 27, No. 1, quoted in Elaine Morgan, *Falling Apart* (London: Abacus, 1978).

9. Shirley du Boulay, *Tutu: Voice of the Voiceless* (London: Hodder & Stoughton, 1988), p. 26.

10. Information taken from www.oxfam.org.uk. See also www.bananalink.org.uk, www.fairtrade.net, www.christianaid.co.uk, www.cafod.co.uk, www.tearfund.co.uk.

11. Jim Wallis, *Faith Works* (London: SPCK, 2002), p. 54.

12. Mick Prentice (see Week Four, One Small Prayer and Two Open Hearts, p. 130).

## Week Two

Opening quotations: Edmund Burke, eighteenth-century Irish politician, and Rosemary Haughton, twentieth-century U.S. theologian: both taken from *The Lion Christian Quotation Collection* (Oxford: Lion, 1997).

1. Philip Pullman, *The Subtle Knife* (New York: Scholastic, 1997), p. 335, spoken through the character of John Parry, ibid, p. 283.

2. Ibid., p. 283.

3. Scientist Peter Atkins, quoted in Russell Stannard, *Science and Wonders: Conversations about Science and Belief,* p. 26.

4. Adam Nathan and Dean Nelson, "Heartbreak behind the Prescott love child," *The Sunday Times,* August 3, 2003.

5. Rowan Williams, *Lost Icons* (Edinburgh: T & T Clark, 2000), pp. 95–7.

6. Anthony Andrew, "Going up in Smoke," *Observer Magazine,* February 22, 2004.

7. Will Provine, quoted in Stannard, *Science and Wonders,* p. 169.

8. Proverbs 3:5–6; 4:18–19, 25–27; 15:10, 16–17, from *The Message* by Eugene H. Peterson (Colorado Springs: NavPress, 1993).

9. Source unknown.

10. Information from various websites including: www.achievement.org, www.girlpower.gov, www.africanamericans.com.

11. Philip Pullman, *The Amber Spyglass,* p. 70.

## Week Three

Opening quotations: Dag Hammarskjöld, twentieth-century Swedish statesman, and Cassiodorus, sixth-century Roman monk: both taken from *The Lion Christian Quotation Collection*.

1. Rowan Williams, *Lost Icons*, p. 40.

2. Robert Winston, *The Human Mind*, BBC TV.

3. Ibid.

4. Carl Jung, quoted in John Polkinghorne, *Science and Providence*, p. 9.

5. Charles Péguy, *God's Dream*—further information on source unknown.

6. Adapted from Romans 15:13.

7. Nick Cohen, "A tale of two cities," *The Observer*, October 19, 2003.

8. Matthew Wall, "Pedal-powered net crusaders," *The Sunday Times*, December 7, 2003.

9. Jhai Foundation www.jhai.org.

10. ww.slowfood.com.

11. John Hooper, "Don't tune in, just turn off," *The Guardian*, Friday, December 12, 2003.

12. Much of this section is taken from "Restoring community in an individualized world," talk by Graham Cray at Greenbelt 2003 (available in recorded form at www.greenbelt.org.uk).

## Week Four

Opening quotations: Evagrius of Pontus, fourth-century writer from Asia Minor (modern-day Turkey), and George Whitfield, eighteenth-century British evangelist: both taken from *The Lion Christian Quotation Collection*.

1. Will Provine, quoted in Russell Stannard, *Science and Wonders: Conversations about Science and Belief,* p. 45.

2. Sam Berry, quoted in ibid., p. 39.

3. John Habgood, quoted in ibid., p. 51.

4. Will Provine, quoted in ibid., p. 61.

5. Richard Dawkins, *The Selfish Gene* (New York: Oxford University Press, 1976), p. 34.

6. Ibid., p. 2.

7. Keith Ward, *God, Chance and Necessity,* p. 137.

8. Richard Dawkins, in an essay entitled "A Devil's Chaplain" in a book of the same name (London: Wiedenfeld & Nicolson, 2003).

9. Will Provine, quoted in Stannard, *Science and Wonders,* p. 61.

10. Richard Dawkins, in "A Devil's Chaplain."

11. Dawkins, *The Selfish Gene,* p. 200.

12. Noam Chomsky, American linguistics scholar, interview in *The Listener,* 1978.

13. Richard Dawkins, in "A Devil's Chaplain."

14. John Pollock, *William Wilberforce* (Oxford: Lion, 1977), p. 75.

15. Ibid., pp. 81–2.

16. Ibid., p. 284 (see www.shonda.org.uk).

17. Ibid., p. 284.

18. For more information on the Shonda Project, contact angela.prentice1@btopenworld.com.

## Week Five

Opening quotations: proverb quoted in *What Katy Did* by Susan Coolidge (New York: Garland Publishers, 1872); Tom Mahon, "The Spirit of Technology," *Wall Street Journal* (January 1996).

1. The actual original quote is from meteorologist Edward Lorenz from a paper presented in 1972 entitled "Does the flap of a butterfly's wings in Brazil set off a tornado in Texas?" from Ziauddin Sardar and Iwona Abrams, *Chaos for Beginners* (Duxford: Icon Books, 1998), p. 54.

2. Ibid., p. 6.

3. Ray Bradbury, "A sound of thunder" in *R Is for Rocket* (Garden City, NY: Doubleday, 1962).

4. Albert Einstein in a letter to Max Born 1926, listed in *Oxford Dictionary of Quotations* (Oxford; New York: Oxford University Press, 1997). Actual quote is, "At any rate, I am convinced that he does not play dice."

5. Ilya Prigogine, *Order out of Chaos* (1984), quoted by Sardar and Abrams in *Chaos for Beginners,* p. 74.

6. An interview with Susan Howatch in *The Sunday Telegraph,* April 1993.

7. Bradbury, "A sound of thunder" in *R Is for Rocket.*

8. Nelson Mandela's inaugural speech, 1994.

9. John Pollock, *William Wilberforce,* p. 50.

10. *Pay It Forward,* directed by Mimi Leder and released by Warner Brothers, 2001.

## Conclusion

Opening quotation is from *The Empty Raincoat* by Charles Handy (London: Hutchinson, 1994).

1. Duncan J. Watts, *Six Degrees: The Science of a Connected Age* (London: Heinemann, 2003), quoted in Steve Poole, "Only Connect," *Guardian Review,* October 18, 2003.

2. Olive Wyon, twentieth-century British writer, taken from *The Lion Christian Quotation Collection.*

3. George Eliot, *Middlemarch,* edited version of ending (U.K.: Penguin Group, 1966), p. 896.

4. Philip Pullman, *The Amber Spyglass,* p. 506.

5. Adapted from Rosemary Conley, *The Flat Stomach Plan* (London: Arrow, 1994).

## Added Extras

Opening quotations: Paul Evdokimov, twentieth-century Russian Orthodox lay theologian, and Origen, second-century Alexandrian scholar and theologian: both taken from *The Lion Christian Quotation Collection.*

1. *Chambers Concise Dictionary* (Cambridge: Chambers, 1989), p. 640.

2. Ibid.

3. Philip Pullman, *The Amber Spyglass,* p. 33.

4. Philip Pullman, *Northern Lights* (New York: Scholastic, 1995) p. 371.

5. Ibid., p. 370.

6. Pullman, *The Amber Spyglass,* p. 74.

7. Ibid., p. 74.

8. Michael Mayne, *Learning to Dance* (London: Darton, Longman & Todd, 2001), p. 50.

9. John Polkinghorne, *Science and Providence,* p. 65.

10. Charles Handy, *The Empty Raincoat.*

11. Source unknown.

12. Luke 15:11–32.

13. Source unknown.

## Leaders' Notes

Opening quotation: source unknown.

1. Adapted from Alice and Walden Howard, Exploring the Road Less Travelled (London: Arrow, 1988), p. 54.

2. C. S. Lewis, *The Last Battle* (Harmondsworth: Puffin, 1956), p. 149.

## About the Author

HILARY BRAND is the author of the bestselling *Chocolate for Lent*, based on the Oscar-nominated movie *Chocolat*. She has also written four children's novels and co-authored *Art and Soul* (IVP), an exploration of faith and the arts. A self-confessed movie junkie, she also loves Scripture and likes seeing what thoughts emerge when the two come together.

The Daughters of St. Paul operate book and media centers at the following addresses. Visit, call or write the one nearest you today, or find us on the World Wide Web, www.pauline.org

**CALIFORNIA**
3908 Sepulveda Blvd, Culver City, CA 90230          310-397-8676
5945 Balboa Avenue, San Diego, CA 92111          858-565-9181
**FLORIDA**
145 S.W. 107th Avenue, Miami, FL 33174          305-559-6715
**HAWAII**
1143 Bishop Street, Honolulu, HI 96813          808-521-2731
Neighbor Islands call:          866-521-2731
**ILLINOIS**
172 North Michigan Avenue, Chicago, IL 60601          312-346-4228
**LOUISIANA**
4403 Veterans Memorial Blvd, Metairie, LA 70006          504-887-7631
**MASSACHUSETTS**
885 Providence Hwy, Dedham, MA 02026          781-326-5385
**MISSOURI**
9804 Watson Road, St. Louis, MO 63126          314-965-3512
**NEW JERSEY**
561 U.S. Route 1, Wick Plaza, Edison, NJ 08817          732-572-1200
**NEW YORK**
150 East 52nd Street, New York, NY 10022          212-754-1110
**PENNSYLVANIA**
9171-A Roosevelt Blvd, Philadelphia, PA 19114          215-676-9494
**SOUTH CAROLINA**
243 King Street, Charleston, SC 29401          843-577-0175
**TENNESSEE**
4811 Poplar Avenue, Memphis, TN 38117          901-761-2987
**TEXAS**
114 Main Plaza, San Antonio, TX 78205          210-224-8101
**VIRGINIA**
1025 King Street, Alexandria, VA 22314          703-549-3806
**CANADA**
3022 Dufferin Street, Toronto, ON M6B 3T5          416-781-9131

¡También somos su fuente para libros,
videos y música en español!